In your face
'Close quarter fighting'

Kevin 0'Hagan 6th Dan

Printed by
New Breed Publishing
Po box 511
Dagenham
Essex RM9 5DN

Reprinted Feb 2004

NEW BREED PUBLISHING WEB SITE AND EMAIL

Web site: www.newbreedbooks.co.uk

Kevin O'Hagans official web site

Bristol Goshin Jutsu Combat Academy

www.4-site.co.uk/goshin/

About the author

Kevin O'Hagan is a professional Martial Arts/Self Protection instructor. He has trained in the Martial Arts for some 28 years now. He holds the rank of 6th Dan black belt in 'Goshin' Ju Jutsu and 1st Dan black in Atemi Jutsu. He is one of the new breed of instructors who are teaching practical Combat Arts and also cross training principles in the UK today. He successfully runs clubs in the Bristol area and is a registered instructor with the British Combat Association, the leading lights in 'real' Self Protection today. Kevin is also a fully qualified fitness instructor and works in the gym's of the local council sports centres. He is also becoming an accomplished writer having written articles for magazines like, 'Fighters', 'Combat' and 'Martial Arts illustrated.' His first book 'I'd thought you'd be bigger' has been received well. This is his second publication to date. Kevin also has also produced a number of his own unique training videos.

October 1998

Copyright Kevin O'Hagan 1998©

Published by

New Breed publishing 1998

No part of this book may be reproduced by any means, nor transmitted, nor translated into machine language, without the written permission of the publisher.

A CIP catalogue record for this book is available from the British Library

Printed and bound in Great Britain.

ISBN 0 9517567 4 5

Please note: The theoretical information and physical techniques outlined in this book are for self-protection and Self defence purposes only. The author and the publishers cannot accept any responsibility for any proceedings or prosecutions brought or instituted against any person or body as a result of the misuse of any theoretical information or physical techniques described in this book or any loss, injury or damage caused thereby.

Dedications

To Mum and Dad for their guidance along the right path

My Children, Thomas, Jacob and Lauren, constant inspiration

Paul Flett my good friend and constant training partner

Thanks as always to Jamie O'Keefe

For Tina for being there

Special thanks to Ray, Ann and Steve for the use of the Bristol

Budokan over the years, sad to see it go

Finally all the students of the Bristol Goshin Jutsu Combat Academy

Foreword
by
Jamie O'Keefe

Foreword by Jamie O'Keefe
'In your face'
'Close Quarter fighting'

When I was approached by Kevin O'Hagan to do a foreword for this book I had to think long and hard about it for a tenth of a second. That's the time it took me to give him my reply, which was yes! And honoured I am that he asked me to.

It shows me that my opinion is regarded as of importance, which gives a special kind of feeling. Although I have written five self protection related books myself; that's an area where I write what I like with complete control over the content matter and the worst thing that could happen is that if people don't like what I have to say, they don't buy my books. Fortunately that's not the case.

Writing this foreword presents a complete different scenario and responsibility. I am not putting the world to rights, giving my opinions and philosophies for the reader to agree or disagree with. My task here is to validate the accuracy of the facts, advice and information given within this publication combined with my own personal testimonial of its author Kevin O'Hagan. With this in mind I now put my finger to the keyboard and hope that I can do justice to such a worthwhile publication.

I think that it can be fair to say that I know Kevin well. In fact I have personally known Kevin for around 20 years since we were both training in traditional martial arts; both searching for that something that seemed to be missing from our respective arts. That something was and is, called 'Self Protection.'

We each followed different paths in our journey; testing, trying, analysing, every aspect of the martial and related fighting systems until we each individually found what we were looking for.

We both ended up at the rank of 6th Dan Black belt and are now regarded as premier league players in the world of self protection. At this level you instinctively know what's 'real' and what's bull!

Kevin is as real as 'real' comes. He knows his stuff. He lives, breathes and eats self protection and is one of the most dedicated self protection participants and instructors that I know of.

Kevin is a serious player who I would certainly like to have by my side if faced with an ugly encounter that I felt uncomfortable dealing with alone. Beside him being a superb martial artist and excellent self protection instructor, he is a really respectful nice guy.

What more can I really say other than that this is the second book that he has written and I would have been proud to have released either of these titles myself. 'In your face' is a superb book which I advise you to read and digest. I am not going to spoil the plot by giving you a breakdown of the books contents because you really do need to read it for yourself. What I will say though is that if you do read it thoroughly. You will find something that might just possibly tip the scales in your favour if you are ever faced with a serious threatening encounter. Just ask yourself now, do you feel 100% comfortable that you can deal with the 'worst of the worst' of situations staring you in the face?

If you rate yourself at 99% capable or below, read this book to gain the other missing percent. Your life and that of your loved ones deserve that extra bit of security.

This is another great book by Kevin and I am proud to associate my name with him.

Stay safe and train as you live.

Jamie O'Keefe 1998. F.S.M.A.
(Founder fellow of the Society of Martial Arts)

PREFACE

PREFACE

"Real" fighting is not the glamorous pastime that is portrayed in the celluloid world of films and video. It is not something that is in any shape or form pleasant, what so ever. Real fighting is frightening, very frightening. It is nasty, scrappy and all too often bloody. It is up close and personal, it is 'In your Face!.

Make no mistake about this, on the streets you will not be sparring or competing, your opponent will not be stancing up or 'bobbing and weaving.'

If you are switched off he will hit you when you least expect it. He will try and catch you with your guard down, he will try to get up close with some verbal approach. Either he will use guile and cunning or pure naked aggression to achieve his aim then he will strike!

In today's violent modern society this is how it is, this is how it happens. You have to get in touch with the rituals, approaches and attackers of today, if you want to stand any chance of beating them.

It's took me a long time to reach these simple conclusions. I have tread many martial paths looking for the truth and to be honest it's been there all the time. From my early experiences of violence at school, around the streets, at football games etc.

I knew deep down what real fighting was like. But when I decided to take up Martial Arts to combat the type of violence I feared I somehow got lost in the misty world of Myth, tradition and ritual. I was learning to fight against stylised attacks and scenarios that just didn't exist in the modern age, yet I carried on because I thought Martial Arts had all the answers and that if the moment of truth came I would be able to execute the techniques I had religiously drilled. Deep down though I still had the nagging doubt whether what I was learning would 'hold up' in a live situation.

I know now from experience that in those early days of my Martial Arts career I was carrying around a very false impression and thought far too highly of my fighting ability, I was treading unsteady territory.

Today I can see it for how it is. With the help of many great instructors and much experience of life, I no longer have any false elusions. I have been there and 'tasted' it and even now will still say I hate violence but a part of me is obsessively and deeply interested in it and I keep on working and honing my skills to combat it. I feel I have come a long way since those early days. I looked for 'reality' and when I found it I must admit part of me didn't much like it but I knew I would have to face these 'new findings' to understand and hopefully master them. I still work every day doing this.

This book is written not only for the people who I know have followed the same journey as me and reached their destination but for others who are hesitant to start the journey. Those who want to know how to begin and maybe also for those denying the truth. As my good friend and one of the UK's leading Martial/self protection instructors Geoff Thompson is fond of saying *'I'll see you when you get there!.'* Good luck.

Kevin O'Hagan 1998

INTRODUCTION
By
Kevin O'Hagan

INTRODUCTION

To prepare yourself for the realities of street combat, you must fully understand that the violent conflict will be up close and personal, it will be literally 'in your face'. When it 'kicks' off, whether it be you using a pre-emptive move or your attacker getting the drop on you, the conflict will take place at 'intimate' distance. You will feel the raw energy of your opponent, see the fear, hate and aggression in their eyes/face, they will also see yours! To precede the conflict there probably will be verbal aggression, swearing, cursing, threats, and intimidation. There is nothing quite like somebody bawling and cursing in a violent rage to set the adrenaline pumping and the knees knocking!

It's at this stage of the encounter where the fight is won. The person who can 'hold their bottle', stand their ground and make the right tactical decision will come out on top. Easy in theory, bloody hard in practice!

So from the verbal, there could also be poking, prodding, pushing, interspersed with remarks like 'C'mon then?' What are you gonna do?' Well? Well? Etc.

These are just a few of the rituals of a street fight situation. Now there are many martial arts out there at the moment claiming they are street orientated or combat effective and I have travelled quite extensively across Britain over the years training and teaching and I can tell you there are only a handful of clubs, teaching and training against the aforementioned tactics/techniques.

The British Combat Association has been foremost in promoting these ideas and anybody within the BCA will know about these concepts but there are still so many that don't and should!

Here are some points to think on:

Most fights do not start by two people sparring off at each other. Normally the person who gets the first good 'shot' in will win. Good street fighters will not let you know when they are going to attack. They will use cunning and guile to sucker punch you. If they think you could be a handful they will use a weapon on you or come mob-handed.

If you don't read a situation right and are not switched on you will be destroyed!

If you don't get a pre-emptive strike off first, they will! It can and will go to grappling very quickly and then to the ground (you should all. know this one by now). Good, clean, rehearsed techniques have a habit of getting very messy in reality.

Nearly all fights start up close (arms length or less). A fourteen stone assailant fuelled on booze will be more than a match for most martial artists.

If your style, system, art, preaches street reality then it must address these problems within it's structure. Although you must train in other aspects too, the majority of your work has got to be at a realistic distance.

No one throws a punch or tries to stab you from 5 feet away! Yet how many are practising their techniques from this distance?

If I had five foot of distance between myself and an assailant armed with a knife I would be doing my running impression of Linford Christie or looking for a suitable makeshift weapon to defend myself with. That's what you do if you have distance and time. When it's in your face you won't have much time or distance. The reality of close quarter combat is brutal and frightening, certainly not glamorous. It will be the time to bring out your personal tried and tested techniques that you know you can perform under pressure, it won't be time for the superfluous or extravagant. It will be time for headbutts, eye gouging, biting, knee stomping, hair pulling, spitting, screaming, shouting and a host of other such pleasantries!

If it goes to grappling expect shirt ripping, tie pulling, coat/jumper pulled over heads, watches being ripped off, stumbling over furniture, kerbs, cars etc, then hard contact with pavements that could be muddy, wet, stoney, littered and cold and uncompromising. Blood, sweat and tears will be spilt down on the floor and huge quantities of energy until your lungs feel like bursting and then some more. You will have to go to the end until there is only one standing. No bells, whistles, refs.

This is what reality based training is about .

If you don't train out such scenarios in your art then it isn't street orientated, Be realistic and honest, don't try and deny this is how it is on the streets .

I started out in martial arts when I was 15 years of age (just a couple of years ago..... OK 20 something years ago) I had great visions of what I could do when blocking that punch coming at me, then countering with the roundhouse kick to the head, then following with that devastating spinning back kick, launching my attacker into orbit !

The first. 'real' encounter after my training saw me under such severe pressure from some wild swinging, puffing and panting opponent that I didn't even have time to get into a stance *(let alone get my shoes off! !)* , then it was on the floor and a big blur of arms and legs, in the end we were both so tired we gave up! I went away at first shocked, confused and wounded (mostly the pride) then I convinced myself it had been a one off and I made a mistake. But as I got older and was exposed to more violence be it on the news, on TV, football violence, riots, pub fights, I began to realise that nobody attacked you like the training partner in the Dojo! No step back before striking, no hands up, no thrust punch or kick and then freeze. It was just wild, naked aggression, a fast blitz of violent energy. I knew then my training and concepts would have to change if I wanted to learn Martial Arts. I feel many others have experienced the same thing, some wake up and get 'real', others still carry on the same old way but know deep down inside that something isn't right. There are many good instructors out there who have been teaching these concepts for years, my Ju Jutsu instructors Mick Upham and David Vincent. Others like David Turton, Jamie O'Keefe and of course Geoff Thompson and Peter Consterdine, not forgetting the formidable late Mr.Gary Spiers.

But for them and instructors alike some times their teaching falls on deaf ears or receives unjust criticism.

OK if you practice martial arts for other reasons bar Self Protection that's fine, that is your choice but then don't go promoting it as 'street orientated', etc. Because unless you are dealing with today's attacker in today's street violence, it will not address self protection in today's world.

I love the martial arts and have participated in most and have the utmost respect for those top in their chosen field. But 1 am also a realist and through many years of personal experience have begun to understand the difference between what you think will work and what does.

In your training you should be practising fast, powerful and accurate strikes to major vital areas. You should train these strikes over and over so you can literally do some with your eyes shut. Practise the strikes or combinations from arms length putting pressure on yourself to put them together with flow. If you fail with one blow, immediately be trained to follow straight in with another and another. Don't plant yourself in a deep stance or be rigid otherwise you won't be able to move quickly. Use every and any natural body weapon available, if one range closes use the next. Use punches, palm heels, hammerfist, knifehands, closer. Work the elbows, forearms, finger jab, clawing, gouging, head and knee strikes, shin kicking, foot stomps, testicles seizing, bites, flesh twisting and pinching. Keep up a continuous assault until the danger is over. If one strike works, great, but train and prepare for continuous and blitzing combinations. In training, time yourself for a twenty or twenty-five second burst of rapid fire strikes. Practise in the air, on the bags, mitts or drill with a partner, this is realistic training for a street orientated encounter.

Also make sure you know how to escape all manner of grabs, holds and chokes if it goes to grappling. Get used to being pulled, pushed, grabbed, choked, lifted, tackled and thrown from upright grappling. Make sure you cover rear grabs, holds etc. as well, don't neglect this as you can't always be switched on a 100%.

Ground grappling? Well, 1 think everything has been said about this over the last few years. Everybody should know the importance of this aspect of combat. Some things to remember though is street grappling is different from submission or mat fighting. In the street you will have to totally incapacitate your opponent not make him tap out!

Atemi (striking) is essential on the deck as equalisers to a larger opponent. A thumb in the eye can get you out of a lot of grappling problems as can a bite.

Also grappling on grass, pavements, tiled floors is very different to grappling on a mat. Try and get some practice on hard and uneven surfaces (be careful), you will find out how vulnerable boney elbows, knees and heads are whilst rolling around on a hard surface.

These are just a few ideas for close quarter fighting. Remember once you have learnt and drilled a move, introduce gradual pressure to make it more realistic.

Close quarter fighting is a fearsome and dangerous affair, where the only rules are no rules and the last man standing wins! I religiously train everyday of the week for this, so I can be prepared, what about you?

'What you don't know will hurt you'.

CONTENTS

About the author
Disclaimer
Dedications
Foreword
Preface
Introduction

Chapter 1 - Attack the attacker.

Chapter 2 - Backs to the wall.

Chapter 3 - Realistic street grappling.

Chapter 4 - Under pressure.

Chapter 5 - Complete control.

Chapter 6 - Escaping the headlock.

Chapter 7 - Palm heel strikes.

Chapter 8 - 2's company 3's a crowd.

Chapter 9 - All systems go.

Chapter 10 - Impact training.

Chapter 11 - Getting to the point.

Chapter 12 - Ambush 'The sneak attack'

Chapter 13 – Visual Scanning to avoid the surprise ambush

Appendices
'A finishing shot'

Chapter 1
Attack the Attacker

"The best defence is a good offence!"
"Action is faster than reaction!"
"Your opponent should feel the strike before he can see it!"

All the above statements are true when we address them to personal combat.

If the Martial Arts system you train in only concentrates on defensive action it is missing a vital element of the overall picture of effective self protection.

We need to practice defensive technique because we may not be always aware, or alert, as we might like, and if somebody gets the drop on you, you will have to know what to do to escape a choke hold, body grab, tackle, or defend against a punch etc. We can't always be ready to command the situation no matter how good a fighter we may be. If suddenly woke from your sleep and you had an intruder leaning over the bed ready to choke you, you would have to know defensive technique.

But some arts practice these principles to the exclusion of anything else. In fact some students believe the only time you react is when they are grabbed, choked or punched. Really in reality this is probably too late. Normally the person to get the first telling blow in will win the encounter.

If you have no choice and we are pushed into the metaphorical corner and you know violence is imminent then you must without clouded judgement attack the attacker with everything you have got.

You must explode with focused and powerful attacks to the vital spots
of your attackers body and escape. This is particularly imperative if your attacker is larger than you, armed or there are more than one,
to delay on your part could be suicidal.

When you know you have no choice, then don't hesitate be fast, be vicious, be first!

We are now going to examine some vital points along with a handful of offensive striking techniques. These are examples and not

cast in stone! Find combinations that suit your body type and size.

Drill them to be instinctive and train them on the heavy bag for impact or realism.

Major K.O. points

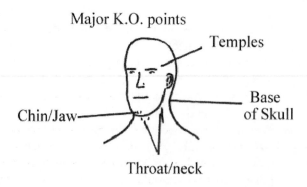

Temples

Base of Skull

Chin/Jaw

Throat/neck

Target - a good strong focused blow to the following spots can cause considerable damage.

Knockout points – Chin/jaw, throat/windpipe, temples, base of skull.

Incapacitating points - Eyes, nose, eardrums, solar plexus, kidneys, groin , kneecaps , biting techniques.

Attitude adjusters/controllers - Shin kicking, elbow dislocating, finger wrenching and breaking, soft tissue/pressure point gouging or ripping, biting.

These are the major and minor weak points, study them, memorise them, every human being no matter how big, strong or muscular will be vulnerable in these areas. Note the knockout points are the ones that can instantly finish a confrontation if struck correctly. The incapacitating areas can stop attacker in his tracks and can be fight stoppers. The last group will give you a distinct advantage and may turn the fight in your favour

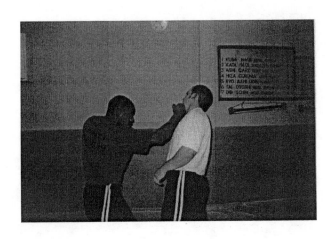

Training Tip:-
Heavy Bagwork is
Essential For
Developing
Striking
Power !

Stickers or
Markers for
Targeting
and
Accurate
Striking !

I believe pre-emptive technique is essential. For most people who are used to dropping into fighting stances and raising their fists, it is hard to adapt to hardly no stance, relaxed posture, verbal disarmament and non-aggressive hand gesturing. All these elements prepare you for a sudden explosive and offensive technique that will take your attacker by complete surprise. You have to do this with a partner and by yourself in a mirror. Check you don't give anything away in your face or body language that your attacker can detect until you suddenly 'blitz' him with your technique ?

When it gets close and you feel your attacker is priming themselves to strike then you prepare to 'go for it'. Rituals of how an attacker prepares to strike you can be found in my book *'I thought you'd be bigger.'* Also I recommend you read Geoff Thompson's excellent book *'The Fence'* and also Jamie O'Keefe's cult classic *'Thugs, mugs and violence'*, to read about how his East end gang would set up a series of crafty tricks and ploys to destroy the opposition, before they even had a clue as to what was happening..

Chapter 2
Back to the Wall

"Fighting your way out of a tight spot."

When the threat of violent confrontation is literally 'in your face' it is a frightening and foreboding feeling. When the seconds begin to tick away and you know there is no place to run or hide you have got to decide very quickly what to do to survive. If you have been cornered and are backed up against a wall, or find yourself in the tight confines of a telephone box or toilet cubicle, then all that martial arts training will flicker through the mind like a hi-tech computer, trying to sort out an appropriate answer to the problem, if takes too long or worse still comes up with the answer 'I haven't trained for this type of scenario, it will all be too late!'

No one likes to be confined or feel restricted, it makes them feel uncomfortable from something like being squashed up against others on a bus, tube or train to having some individual actually corner you and threaten violence.

In my younger days I can remember on many occasions being cornered and held up. I lived in a multi-racial neighbourhood, where there were many street gangs or notorious families. As a kid I dreaded walking down the street in case one of these 'said' people would suddenly pounce and demand my 'pocket money' or wait to see what I had in my bag or throw challenging questions like **'what football team do you support?'** or **'what school do you go to'**

You knew if the answer you gave wasn't the 'right' one there would be trouble and there usually was. The amount of times it happened in my youth I can't re-count from simply being pushed against a wall, to multiple crowding, to having a knife poked to the belly.

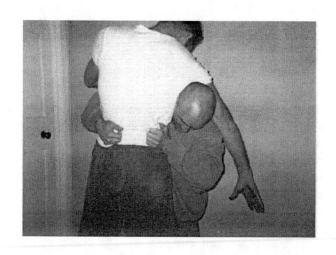

I've experienced it all and I have experienced that feeling of total helplessness and fear and that eminent feeling of impending violence.

When I was younger I also enjoyed going to football matches, every Saturday it was a regular thing throughout the 70's and early 80's. But the sickening violence I became exposed to in mass confines of crowds was terrifying. You can be standing innocently one moment watching the game, the next you can be swept along in a tide of bodies and crushed up against a wall, fighting for air. I have many a bad memory of these things! All these experiences of being cornered and backed up made me think once I started training in martial arts that l wanted to learn how to get out of those situations.

I wanted to no longer feel helpless or vulnerable when backed up or crowded in. I wanted my chosen art to answer for me what happens when some thug bursts into a telephone box when you're using it and sticks a knife in my face and demands money, or what do I do when coming out of a pub toilet to be confronted in the restricted and closed in area.

Most martial arts systems don't have the answers, most don't even practise these scenarios. It took me many years of searching and also personal training before I got the answers. The bottom line in my experience is if you can't fight close up you have got major problems.

You can have the most devastating kicks in the world, the most large powerful dynamic throws, superb reverse punches but when someone has their hands around your throat pressing you hard against a wall , where you can feel their breath in your face and see the hate in their eyes it ain't going to help you.

The same as any other aspect of martial arts. if you want to be proficient at it, you have got to practise it regularly.

Get your training partner to stick you up against a wall, push you into a corner. If you get a chance use the real environment of a telephone box, a lift, stairway, etc, and play out the scenarios and see what you can come up with . Try it against an unarmed attacker, then against a knife hold-up and then against more than one attacker. Try to re-create the pressure, fear and adrenaline rush of a real confrontation and see how you handle it , it's a good tester and 'yard stick' for a 'live situation.'

Obviously being cornered isn't a good option if you have others but remember, find some positives out of the situation.

With your back up against the wall no-one can come from behind you. You can use the wall to brace yourself, to launch an attack, you can also 'turn the tables' and use the wall angles to your advantage with quick foot work to get yourself out of a tight spot.

If you ever played draughts and your last piece is cornered by the 'Kings' you will know there is a certain position in the corner of the board that will prevent you getting caught out and you can move in and out all day, as in turn there is a wrong one also, that will finish you! Also it may well be worth studying tapes of boxers and see how they fight out of a corner, or with their backs to the ropes and see how they can turn the situation around. Men like Mohammed Ali and 'Sugar' Ray Leonard were masters of this, of course not all the ring tactics will stand up in the street situation but they can help.

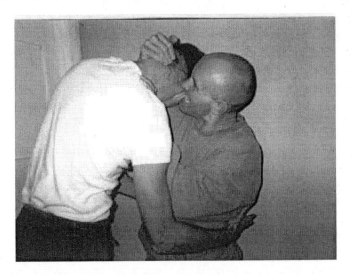

So what are some of the things you can do when 'backed up' and you have got to fight your way out.

If you are against a wall or pushed against it, if you have the distance before the opponent closes it down , thrust a low hard front or side kick into their advancing kneecap to stop them in their tracks, then using the wall as a brace catapult yourself off it rapidly and smash a horizontal elbow strike into their head, grab or clinch them and fire a few rapid fire knees into the groin and abdomen, then pull their head down to knee, or you might from this position step to the side and ram their head into the wall to finish the encounter.

Again if you are pushed up against a wall, door, etc, launch yourself forward with your best hand strike, whether it be a right cross, left hook, palm heel, elbow or spear hand, fire it in and make it count, then make your escape. If it were two opponents closing you down, try a rapid knee stomp to one and an explosive hand strike to the other aiming for chin, eyes or throat, then get out quick. These moves will all depend on your quick decisive action.

If the attacker grabs you up close by your jacket, shirt, etc, brace your back against wall then slap your open palms over his eardrums for an instant concussion, a follow up double thumb gouge to the eyes or a short head butt to the nose will get you out of trouble. Also in a close up grab you can grab the short hairs on the side of the head or the ears to twist and control then follow up with a head butt or some rapid fire knees to groin, solar plexus or outer thigh. Spear fingering the eyes or windpipe will get you a reaction, as will stomping the instep and kicking the shin bones.

Don't overlook gripping and squeezing the testicles or biting into face, ear, neck, or any other exposed body target to set up an escape.

If you find yourself being strangled and pushed up the wall by a one handed choke, rapidly break attackers extended elbow joint with your forearm in a scissor like action. If strangled with both hands come up between the arms and grip assailants windpipe with a claw hand grip and pin them into the wall, follow up with knee strikes to the groin, then sweep the legs away.

If you go to a clinch try twisting and squeezing the flesh surrounding the kidneys (clothing allowing this), then use a close quarter front shin kick to the groin, before either inner or outer sweeping the legs away or working your way behind opponent by upper-cutting and hooking the ribs/kidneys or biting the body to get on a choke or strangle hold or reaching between assailants legs to squeeze the testicles and throw him into the wall. If opponent hits the wall face first follow up with hook punches to kidneys, or a knee to the spine or palm heel, elbow or forearm to the base of the skull. All these moves are quick and highly effective, the wall will give you good balance. Also when facing opponent don't overlook spitting into his face (if you have any saliva) or using any makeshift implement like throwing loose change in face, a handkerchief, keys or wallet to distract and set up your counter attack.

If you can use the environment around you don't hesitate. If in a phone box slam the receiver down on bridge of attackers nose, or crash it down on a grabbing hand. In a toilet cubicle slam their heads into the door, fingers in door hinges if possible or if you are caught in the act urinate on them!!, what ever it takes;

overlook no possibilities! The list is only limited by the imagination.

Another method of training is against a heavy six foot punch bag. Get up real close to it and don't move back, fire in rapid and continuous elbows, knees, short hooks and uppercuts, headbutts, short sweeping kicks with the inside edge of foot at shin height and also use short palm heels, clawing, gouging and biting (don't damage the bag!) Also clinch the bag, work your way behind it and fire blows to the imaginary rear targets and practise chokes as well as short sweeps.

Also good drills for stamina is to do three minute rounds just using elbows; then one using just knees, or another grabbing the bag with one arm and just fire short hook punches with the free hand for one minute continuous no stopping, then swoop and use other arm. During these moves slip in a few head and shoulder strikes as well.

These are a few of the many drills and techniques you can train in and if you want to feel comfortable up close you must train at it constantly putting yourself in the worst possible scenarios and finding a way out.

In closing remember a wild animal is at it's most dangerous when cornered, so can you be with the right training!

Chapter 3
Realistic Street Grappling
'Going to ground, a good option?'

With the sudden wave of interest in ground grappling techniques sweeping through the Martial arts world, it may be interesting just for a brief moment to sit back and read this chapter.

Hopefully it can shed some light on just where ground grappling fits into the Combat Martial artists repertoire of techniques and also it's strengths and weaknesses, plus what is essential to know if you go to the floor in a fight!

Firstly just look again at the last few words of the above paragraph. **'If you go to the floor in a fight'**, what I mean is a real street situation not a Judo, Wrestling or Ju Jutsu contest or match. Floor grappling in the street is a whole different world to any form of contest no matter how **'no holds barred'** it is, it is just not the same.

Let's look at the major differences between the 'street' techniques and those seen being executed in a ring, or contest area, which will not necessarily hold up in a real situation.

Firstly let's get it straight, the floor is the last place you want to be in a 'live' street fight. It is an extremely dangerous and vulnerable position to be in, the bottom line is avoid going to the 'deck' unless you have no other choice. Why? Well look at the negatives. Number one, ground grappling may be strong against a one to one opponent but if he has a weapon, or there is more than one opponent, it could be suicidal. Number two, when two opponents are rolling around on the floor any onlookers, no matter how impartial they may be, suddenly get the urge to 'pitch in', they will start either kicking away at one or the other person on the ground (normal in this situation, either of the two will pick up the damage) or they might decide to batter the 'top' man with a chair, bar stool, dustbin lid (depending on where the fight may be), even worse they may come in at an exposed back with a knife or a broken glass or bottle.

Another scenario is for some 'hero' to rush over and proceed to pull the two combatants apart, then usually one gets a good shot and the other or we have a third person to the fight and then all hell can break loose. A crowd 'fired up' can be like a rabid pack of dogs! It is a very frightening situation and I have experienced this from being in crowds at football matches when trouble has erupted, and I tell you on the floor is not the place to be. Thirdly think of environment (No not if the ozone layer is still deteriorating) but where you might be if you hit the deck. Remember most grappling arts like Judo and Wrestling are done on mats or canvas, so you have no fear of hitting the ground. Arts like the now famous Brazilian Ju Jutsu were practised in a warm climate country where the exponents fought on sandy beaches, lush grassland. They were not rolling around on an icy, hard, cold, uneven and uncompromising pavement in the middle of January on a winter night, nor was it designed for thrashing around on a beer soaked or glass covered bar floor or dance floor after trouble has started or neither for struggling on a urine drenched toilet floor!

Remember, if you are out for a quiet night with your 'lady', with your best 'designer' gear on, looking cool, the last thing you want to be going is rolling about in three different kinds of dog excrement (note how I cleaned that up, I wish someone would!) in front of the local 'takeaway'.

So hopefully by now you can see some of the down points to floor grappling. Also to be considered is the time factor, the longer you are on the floor the more dangerous it becomes for you.

Wrestling and Judo pins are not much good in 'real combat' they can only serve as time buying 'manoeuvres' to get into a better finishing technique. In the street you will not be looking for an opponent to 'tap out' and submit, you will be looking for a quick finish and get back onto your feet, it won't be a timed bout with the 'ref' ready to step in. An opponent who may submit to a hold or lock can and may get up and suddenly up the stake by drawing a weapon or fashioning one out of something at hand. It really is best to make sure he doesn't get up again in a hurry so you can make your exit!

So what do I do if I go to the floor? Well there's plenty but the rule of the street is make it quick, don't let your opponent settle into a good hold or get into a superior position.

The following techniques, concepts and theories are taken from the system of Martial Arts I teach 'Kempo Goshin Jutsu', they have worked for me in and out of the dojo, they are not by any means unique but they are what I teach my students to do on the floor, remember **'how you train, is how you react'**. I believe if you don't have command of the following techniques you will struggle badly on the floor, especially against a large and aggressive opponent.

These techniques are an overview, not the whole picture, otherwise it may take a whole book to demonstrate these!

If you go to the ground and you are on top of opponent, cushion your fall by landing on them. There is a certain sickening feeling about landing on a pavement on your kneecaps or elbows.

Try and drive your knee into their groin and then fall, dropping the point of your elbow into the sternum (breastbone) or solar plexus. Naturally from there let your head snap forward in a butt to their face, best target the nose.

Climb so you straddle their chest, consolidate your balance and bang away with fist, elbows, palm heels and butts, then get out quick. If pulled down close by opponent immediately bite into nose, ear, cheek or neck for a release then gouge into the windpipe with a claw hand squeezing it shut or thumb gouge into the eyes or ram fingers up their nostrils and rip. Grabbing the hair or ears and banging the head on the floor has quite a 'sobering' effect on your would be attacker, so has a fast choke hold.

If you feel you are losing balance in this 'mount' position lean over and rest hands on floor put your chest into opponents face, when he pushes you off take his straight arm pivot off his chest to the side and dislocate the elbow with the famous cross armbar (Jujugatame), make sure you drive the heel of your armlocking feet into the face and body of your opponent to prevent them attempting biting your leg.

If you go down underneath, then get opponent between your legs in 'the guard' position. If he attempts to punch you, pull him forward in the scissors until he loses balance, pull his head down to yours and bite into his ear, get one of your feet between his legs and flip him over and off.

If he is strangling you push back with your legs and hips, grab his straightened arm, swing your foot over his neck and pull him over and down for the cross arm bar again.

If he has mounted your chest and is choking you, drive your thumbs up into his eyes, then grab the back of his head and his chin and crank his neck around in a hard twist to take him off your body.

Gouging or finger thrusting into the Jugular Notch (the indentation at the base of the windpipe) is a good move, as is ripping the side of his mouth with your thumbs or digging a knuckle into the mastoid behind the ear. Combine these with butts, then twist the opponent off you.

If opponent is on his stomach and you straddle his back, hit him with elbows and shoot punches to spine and back of neck. If he attempts to push himself up, then go straight for a choke or kneel on the back and pull up on his chin to finish.

If you are lying sideways across opponent's body and he has your neck locked then grab and squeeze his testicles or pinch flesh high on his inner thigh, also push your boney forearm into his neck or up under his nose to relieve pressure then bite his body anywhere (nipples, pec's, flesh on floating ribs) until you can get out.

When you are under in the same position, hammer away at his exposed kidneys and floating ribs, get a hand under and between his to squeeze testicles and bite at any exposed target, then twist out and get on top. The list could go on and on but hopefully this will show you the different sort of technique and mental attitude you need for 'street wrestling', these moves are equalisers especially for smaller people. I know loads of armbars, locks, leg locks, strangles etc, but in a street situation you will not have the time to execute them, you have got to adapt. Refer to my book 'Grappling with reality' for more details.

Some may say the moves are brutal, but in answer to that, unless you have experienced a situation where your strength is ebbing, your arms feel like lead, your guts feel sick and you have a larger, heavier and stronger opponent lying on you, you will have to know and use the techniques mentioned.

One of my regular training partners and fellow instructor used to be a 14 stone plus PTI in the prison service. He is a good grappler and a hard opponent, he made me work and took me to the limit of physical endurance, which is great because I know my techniques will get me out along with good physical conditioning (which is essential in ground grappling) and mental stamina.

How many instructors out there grapple or spar or whatever with their instructors or students? You will learn a lot about yourself, your belt or position won't matter once it goes down.

Win or lose you will learn, if you are prepared to give it a go!

In the street the attacker will not give a darn who you are and when it goes to the floor you will have to separate contest grappling and street grappling to survive. I hope this chapter has gone some way to explaining this.

'It isn't important to come out on top, what matters is to come out alive'. Bertolt Brecht - Jungle of cities.

Chapter 4
'Under Pressure'

'Keeping your head in a fight!'

Learning Defences against a punch to the head is taught in just about every martial art and fighting system. Techniques go from the simple to the highly intricate. Each art has it's own ideas and methods. People who take up the martial arts are eager to learn these skills as punching attacks are probably the most commonly used street attack. But with all the theories and techniques at our disposal is it such a simple job to block, parry, trap, etc, and return a counter against a head punch.

I have been involved in the martial arts some 28 years now and have been teaching for 15 of these, I have travelled around teaching and have made some observations on the subject.

Firstly I will state in a street situation when a verbal argument turns to physical, a seasoned fighter who knows how to set you up and is the master of the 'sucker punch' will have hit you before you know it, unless you are also tuned into how the street assailant will punch you. If you don't know the signs and you are not switched on all the techniques in the world will not help you.

A hefty blow to the jaw/chin or temple will have you all over the place if not 'down and out'.
I have found a lot of martial artists are practising punch defences from an unrealistic distance, four to five feet away is not a realistic distance. A person will need to be at least three feet or nearer to effectively throw a good punch and note; so will you!

If you had five foot distance, why be waiting to block/counter, you could use a 'stop hit' as JKD people refer to, in this case a crushing low line kick to the shin, knee or thigh, why root yourself to the spot and block!

In a street scenario very rarely do you get somebody spar up to you, ready to exchange blows. The street thug doesn't want to slug it out for 6 x 3 min. rounds, he wants to separate you from your senses with one big shot, usually an overhand right, or wild swinging haymaker or a type of hook. He will not take a boxers stance, nor will he step back into classical stance, hand pulled back to hip.

He will verbally disarm you and take his shot from where he stands, no ritualistic posing, just 'bang' !

You won't have time to step back into stance, anyway if you do you will be on the back foot and he will swarm you with punches.

Remember he won't be imitating the famous 'one arm syndrome', where one punch is thrown and he freezes in place while you dismantle him! If his first shot misses or is blocked he will follow up with another and another.

Most classical blocking methods fall short when applied against a 'street puncher' or 'boxer'. Inner, outer and rising blocks become redundant, 'X' blocks suicidal. Committed punches with body weight behind them and the opponent not holding back will crash through these blocks, taking into account if you even get time to attempt to use one. 'Live' fighting is not rigid one, two, three motions, it is fast, furious and continual motion.

In regard to blocking in general, how many blocks do you see executed in a boxing match, how many have you seen in the 'no holds barred' contest? Even 'high level exponents of the hard Shotokan Karate style when competing in point karate tournaments are hardly ever seen using the classical blocks! That should tell you something!

In 'real' punching range all you will have is instinctive reaction blocks or better termed as cover ups. The moves are reminiscent of how a boxer may cover up against blows, but just slightly modified.

Let's take the first example: You are confronted by trouble and sense your aggressor is going to strike. You should have stepped back into a small 45% stance, let's say left leg leading. Ideally if you .feel an attack on your person is imminent, you should 'kick off', with your own offensive attack but this may not always be possible for one reason or the other. So suddenly the attacker throws s big overhand right or hook. You will have to bring your hands up instinctively, left hand covering the left side of your head. I call this a 'telephone' block, the position resembles the way your hand/arm is when holding the receiver of a phone to your ear. The punch can be taken on the forearm or if it is hooking around your bicep and shoulder can absorb the strike (refer to photograph).

The cover up is a natural reaction, you don't have to go into any sophisticated ritual before you execute it. (*As brilliantly described in Jamie O'Keefe's knife fights in Thugs, mugs and violence*).

People have lots of inbred reflex actions, that with the right training can be used without much conscious pre-thought. For example, if somebody shouted **'look out'**, or **'duck'**, your body naturally crouches without conscious effort. This is how the cover up block should be done, if you train it, it begins to make good sense.

If performed correctly you should stop that blow but also be at a good distance to immediately counter. Make sure your non-blocking hand is up in a guard position and not by the hip.

With the hand up in guard you can instantly strike back or block another punch coming in. What you follow up with is up to you and how you see fit, as long as your head is still on your shoulders, you can fight back!

Now if you were initially in the left stance and this time the aggressor threw a left hook, you can either bring up your right hand in the 'telephone block', or you can pivot your hips and come across to meet the punching arm with a modified double knifehand block with your left, smashing into their wrist and bicep, from there you can 'shoot' back with a reverse knifehand to neck, hammerfist to jaw, slap to eardrum, elbow to jaw etc. The important element is you haven't changed stance, so if you face somebody and you don't know if they are going to punch you with the right or left hand, you will have a chance because you are not shuffling your feet, looking for the correct stance!

The principle was taught to me some 12 years ago by my then Ju Jutsu instructor and it is one of the fundamental tactics of the Kempo Goshin Jutsu system that I teach. It is common-sense, but in my experience of teaching, very few others practise it. It is essential to have any hope of blocking a punch.

Against a flurry of Swings you should again cover up the head with the 'telephone blocks' either side, then come up the middle with a knee strike to assailants groin/body or headbutt to the face, you will also be in a position of 'inside control' to grapple or throw if you so wish.

Learning to duck or 'bobweave' under a haymaking swing is worth practising, you can evade the blow and come up on the outer side of the attacker to punch the ribs/kidneys or go for the rear choke or strangle.

Also slipping and parrying straight punches over your shoulders is a smart but fairly advanced idea but again worth investing time in.

To learn how to effectively cover, slip, duck, etc, practice against a partner with the 'gloves on', start off easy, don't blast away otherwise you do not develop the necessary technique, reflexes and confidence needed. Don't make the mistake of only punching in a sparring scenario, you must practice the face off, confrontational scenarios where nine times out of ten it will happen. Work the drills, practice against the different punches and learn your different defences Gradually build up to full power shots and pressurise yourself. You will find how difficult stopping punches really is, you will probably stop more with your face when you start off!

Other tips to consider when facing an aggressor and you feel he may attempt a punch are as follows: always try and maintain arms length distance, this will give you some chance of seeing the blow.

Try not to get your mind or attention distracted otherwise you will be sucker punched. Don't go into 'stupid' pre-fight rituals like standing head to head or splaying arms, hands on hips, puffing out the chest! these actions leave you no hope of defending whatsoever.

Also be aware of the pre-punch signs. Opponent may be wildly abusive, finger point, attempt to prod or push you. May suddenly go quiet, have a vacant stare or look; (this may be difficult to spot on some gormless individuals), blood red face, veins protruding from temples or neck, clenching of fists, drop of shoulders, draw back of arm, shift of bodyweight, These are just some of the many different approaches. Be aware of these things they are just as essential, if not more than your physical responses. Remember the street thug will not stance up and start dancing around like 'Sugar Ray Leonard'. These are not the things you should be looking for, or base all your punch training on. You may be accosted in a telephone box, toilet cubicle, stairway, car etc.

It probably won't be of your choice! You must accept these things and take them on board!

In closing the best defence is attack, and if you can launch a pre-emptive move even when you feel your life is threatened, do it, don't delay and find yourself on the back foot. But if something goes wrong and you can't then by following the concepts outlined in this chapter, you will be able to 'keep your head' !

Training Tip

Keep opponent at Arms length

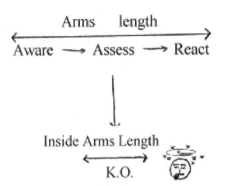

Arms   length

Aware ⟶ Assess ⟶ React

Inside Arms Length

K.O.

None of the above principles can be applied!

No time !

Chapter 5
Complete control Neck-locks, chokes and strangles for Combat

'Control the head and the body will follow!'

In the animal kingdom every beast is inbred with the instinct when life is in danger to go for the 'jugular' and attack the neck and 'throat' area to end a confrontation quickly.

In the human world of serious combat, or street-fighting conflict, a trained exponent of the 'real' martial arts will have the same animal instinct to attack the most vulnerable area on the human body, the throat/neck area.

Attacks to the throat and neck can be lethal in their nature and just be reserved for life threatening dangers like, for instance, if you are attacked by a weapon wielding attacker, if you are faced by multi-assailants or if it is a rape situation and also if your opponent is so much larger than you or totally and violently dangerous. When you face the conflict of any of the previous mentioned scenarios then you will be glad to have the knowledge of how to attack the throat/neck.

Let's look a little closer at the structures of the neck and see how susceptible the; can be.

Air is breathed in through the nostrils and passes to the back of the throat where it enters the trachea (windpipe). The trachea is a tube of cartilage about four to five inches long situated at the front of the neck and leads into the chest and divides into two branches, one for each lung. The air travels to the lungs where an exchange of gases takes place.. Here, the oxygen is taken up by the blood. Carbon dioxide - bearing air is then expelled as we breathe out.

If the airway is interfered with in any way and air cannot pass through, the brain will indirectly be starved of oxygen and unconsciousness can result. It can be done in many ways, a blow with the edge of the hand (knifehand) is a powerful and lethal atemi strike, also the closed fore-knuckle driven into The trachea can stop anyone in their tracks, as can the stiffened finger tips thrusted into the jugular notch (the small indentation at the base of the throat).

Just by pushing in and down on this vital spot with the fingers or thumb can immediately break any frontal hold on you, even when grappling on the floor. At close range a heavy elbow or forearm strike can instantly drop the most determined attacker when driven in against the Thyroid Cartilage (Adam's Apple) or larynx (voice box).

Choke holds from the front and rear can be used to compress the windpipe. From the rear the radius bone (thumb side) of wrist is shoved against throat then joined up with the other hand to execute the choke. This can be done in many fashions. From the front, a claw hand grip onto either side of the trachea can effect a nasty little choke that can be turned into a lethal move by ripping and pulling the trachea out.

Another area on the neck are the Carotid Arteries. These run up the side of the neck vertical with the trachea. You have the Common carotid arteries which at the level of the Adam's Apple branch off into the internal and external carotid arteries, internal supplying blood to the brain, external supplying the face and scalp. Where they branch this point is known as the Carotid Sinus. If this point is struck with the edge of the hand, the blood flow to the brain will be disrupted and unconsciousness will occur.

Strangleholds which involve both carotid arteries being squeezed between your forearm and biceps result in a 'sleeper hold' where you have drastically slowed the flow of blood rich in oxygen to the brain, result a blackout. This is superb technique against a drug-crazed attacker who may be impervious to kicks, punches or joint locks. Again this hold can be applied from rear, side or front, standing or on the ground in many various ways.

The final vulnerable area is the cervival vertabrae at the base of the skull. Having the neck severely wrenched or twisted can damage the vertebrae possibly breaking the neck.

From the front, the back of the head and chin can be grabbed and the neck/head twisted around, even the biggest of assailant will go with this for fear of the damage it can do. When the assailant is on the floor you can straddle their back or kneel on it and then clasp your hands under their chin and pull up the head putting extreme pressure on the neck. This is an excellent controlling technique.

Once more, these neck-locks, head cranks and twists can be executed in a multitude of ways or combined with the chokes and strangles or followed on from an atemi blow.

The holds can he applied with the legs as well as the hands when on the floor in a grapple.. The legs can perform guillotine chokes where the head gets caught and crushed between thigh and calf or scissor like choke holds, triangle leg locks to the neck or many neck cranks and crushes. The legs are powerful weapons. The list could go on and on, these are just a few examples.

I have taught many people the value of these techniques in life threatening situations from housewives and mums in self defence classes to army, security, bodyguards and doormen who may have to resort to these moves in the 'line of duty'.
The beauty of these moves are that they can instantly control a larger opponent or literally drop them in their tracks no matter how tough they might be. Also psychologically when you go for the throat it will 'freak' an attacker out and let him know you mean business. Plus there is a horrible feeling of panic and helplessness when you are subjected to a choke or strangle.

I speak from training experience, a most undesirable position to be in.

On a topical note; in the ultimate fighting championships which is as near as you will get to real conflict with minimum rules, most of the fights have ended with chokes, strangles or neck-locks. This shows just how effective and versatile they can be.

If you wish to know more about these techniques, you may wish to read my book **'I thought you'd be bigger'** where I have gone into more detail.

IN THE ANIMAL WORLD, EVERY PREDATOR GOES FOR THE NECK !

Chapter 6
Escaping the Headlock

'Grapplings most common hold'

One of the most common grappling attacks in the street, or the controlled arena, is the headlock, in some shape or form.

To the skilled exponent it can be a powerful finishing technique when executed correctly. To the unskilled it is a hold they seem to naturally slip into during the course of a struggle at grappling range, whether it be standing or on the ground.

Sometimes the headlock is referred to as the 'schoolboy' hold because I imagine that everybody at one time or another were caught in this hold in the playground or executed it on someone else!

Even the roughly applied version of this hold can be dangerous and will give you problems escaping. The side headlock when clamped on can constrict the carotid arteries running up the side of the neck and slow blood Flow down to the brain, making a 'sleeper hold'. Also if the head is trapped with one hand the attacker can pound away with their free hand to your face, causing considerable damage .

You can also be thrown heavily to the floor and be pinned in a worse position. There is also a danger of your attacker 'running' you in the side headlock - head first - into a wall, door, table edge, etc, etc.

The front headlock can become a powerful choke to the windpipe or a severe neck crank if twisted.

Fortunately most untrained fighters will just roughly squeeze or hold the head/neck while trying to manoeuvre you into a strike. If you react in the early stages of the holds you can have a good chance of escape even from a much larger and stronger opponent. The longer you leave it the harder it will become to escape and even the novice fighter may succeed in securing a strangle or choke on you.

We will look at a few methods of escapes from the side and front headlocks. I have used these in 'live' situations and in 'pressure tests' in the dojo and nine times out of ten they have worked. Hopefully they may help the novice grappler in defending these holds.

As the Side headlock is applied you can immediately drop your inside hand up and over the attackers shoulder and either pull back on the hair, claw eyes, rip up nostrils or hook the mouth, at the same time your other hand can grab and squeeze the testicles or pinch the flesh high on the upper thigh. As grip begins to slacken on you, hook behind their knee and lift up and tilt them up and back for a throw. If opponent is too heavy to lift, fall back with them and immediately start atemi, striking any vital body part that is open, then escape.

If opponent hangs on to you after the lift and throw, settle your body weight and get a foot over their body to stop them pulling you across theirs. Then grind your forearm into their neck or jaw line or knuckle press the mastoid cavity behind ear, or gouge at an eye to break hold from around your neck. When broken you can escape or finish with a lock or strike of your own.

Again from the standing side headlock you have other options. If your head is pulled tightly in opponent's chest, turn your head and sink your teeth into the pectoral muscle and bite hard, this will give you a release. Dropping to your knee and bringing up a stiff forearm blow to the groin from the rear can complete the move.

Alternatively your front hand can finger spear to opponent's eyes if they have been careless with their own head position, or you can uppercut/hook punch their groin, simple but effective moves (usually the best).

If you reach behind opponent's back you can hook/clamp their free arm and wrist to prevent them punching you. If you keep your forearm tightly clamped to their backs it is very hard for them to break free from your grip.

A pure Ju Jutsu technique that can work as a surprise move goes like this: if opponent headlocks you low and drops their weight you can reach and grab their groin from the front, step your front foot around between their legs, and drop for a rolling throw taking opponent across your falling body to the floor, you will end up on top of them where you can finish with strikes etc.

The front headlock again can be foiled early with an uppercut punch, forearm or grab to testicles, this works well.

Many years back I trained with members of the Israeli anti-terrorist squad on a special course. Part of the training was to pressure test you by free fighting bare handed with no rules, anything goes (I don't recommend this to everyone!). During my 'fight' I was caught in a front headlock by one of these Israelis, who politely whispered in my ear in broken English *'If you struggle, I break your neck'* (nice chap). I immediately shot in the groin punch followed by a grab which broke up a very tight hold. He did succeed in opening a cut under my eye as he tried to gouge it on the way out (like I said, nice chap!) but I was out and fit to fight another day!

Again bites will work a treat. If you first grip and squeeze the flesh on the back of thigh and kidneys you can loosen up the hold long enough to turn your head and bite the body. From there you can 'shoot' for the legs to execute a takedown, where you can follow up.

If you are taken to your knees with this hold you must keep grabbing for the groin and look for an opening to escape or grab and break a finger to aid your counter. If you go to the floor with a skilled grappler in a headlock you will have problems if you don't immediately make a move. Once they settle into one of these holds it can be near on impossible to escape.

There are many different floor escapes, but really are out of the scope of this chapter. If you want to learn these techniques then seek out a good Judo, Ju Jutsu or grappling instructor who will show you.

But in overview if you react early look to gouge for eyes, nose, mouth, attack throat or groin or bite any available target, this should give you some sort of opening.

In closing let me emphasise again that the headlocks are extremely common in fights whether it be a mugging or a one to one encounter.

If you are serious about defending yourself on the streets and being a well rounded martial artist you must learn to defend these holds to have any sort of chance.

Good luck in your training.

Survival Tip
Remember grappling is a last resort
Avoid it if you can!

Chapter 7
Palm Heel Strike

'Underestimated striking power'

Within every martial arts systems are striking or Atemi-waza technique. Some concentrate on one or two particular strikes and build their system around it, e.g. punching, karate or boxing and others like 'Kempo' use many different and diverse Atemi blows.

One very simple but explosive hand blow is the 'palm heel' strike, sometimes overlooked in favour of the standard fist.

It's power is often underestimated as is it's versatility. It takes minimum training to learn how to form and hit with the palm heel, yet it guarantees immediate results.

The fist as a striking weapon, on the other hand, requires many, many hours of work to refine and get right. Most people think they can punch, but when they come up against the heavy hag or focus pads they suddenly discover all the pitfalls and realise they don't carry dynamite in their fists!

Boxers spend hour upon hour practising hitting with body weight behind their blows, with speed and accuracy. As a weapon of self defence the fist can be fragile and prone to injury. Look at a fearsome puncher like 'Mike Tyson', even he in a street altercation some years back, broke a bone in his right hand when landing a punch to his opponent's head. If this can happen to the mighty Tyson how would the average person fare?

Smashing your fist into an opponent's boney skull or elbows is bad enough with gloves on, bare fisted on the streets it's like hitting a brick wall! You can sustain broken hand bones, sprained wrists, dislocated fingers and broken or badly damaged knuckles. It may see you having to fend off an attack one handed.

Again boxers wrap, tape and glove their hands when they fight in the ring, not just to minimise damage to their opponent but to minimise injury to their own hands. Still many end up with the above mentioned injuries even then!

Also in the UFC fights where bare knuckle punching is allowed, a vast majority of fighters pulled out with hand damage and also note the distinct lack of KO's with the fists in these bouts.

You may now think I am anti punching. Far from it, I love punching, boxing and work regularly on my punching technique. But for self defence I prefer the palm heel because you are less prone to injury and you can inflict terrible damage with the heel of the hand.

I know there are prolific punchers who have made punching work in and out of the Dojo, and I have felt their power first hand

e.g. Geoff Thompson and Mr. Peter Consterdine, but these guys, and others like them are the exception to the rule. Fighting bare knuckled is a whole different world to gloved fighting.

The average person looking for a good strike for self protection should explore and practise the palm heel.

Do you doubt it's effectiveness? Read the classic combat texts Get Tough by Fairbairn, Kill or get Killed by Applegate and Cold Steel, Styers. These tough combat veteran men, who between them dealt with much live action, all sing the praises and recommend the use of the palm heel or 'chin jab' as they refer to it in a combat situation.

I have taught this blow to many different people and found they have adapted quickly and found confidence in it. Young children can pack a surprise blow with it to foil an assailant when they attempt to pick them up. A good shot under the nose, even from a child can hurt like hell and force a release. Lady students in self defence classes take to the palm heel with relish and after testing it on the focus pads they find out how potent it can be slammed into the chin, jaw or nose! I have also taught elderly people, the merits of the heel hand and both groups, after a little training, could well pack a surprise for a would be mugger! The confidence this simple strike gives is wonderful to see. Timid or shy people who come to train suddenly find they have got a natural weapon that can really work with the right training.

Why is it such a powerful blow? Because it utilises one of the bodies hardest natural points. The thick mass of bone at the base of the palm and the wrist junction doesn't need any prior conditioning either to use as a fist does.

Sometimes when teaching the palm heel I like to say to my students 'who fancies going over and punching the Dojo wall with their fists? (most are reluctant) I liken the wall to someone's bony skull. Then I say 'if I asked you to palm heel that wall would you feel better about it?' Again most say yes!

This willingness to use the blow will help them in a self defence situation simply because they won't feel they're holding back due to fear of injury which the punch might bring. This I feel makes it an all round strike for everybody regardless of age.

I have taught this blow as part of my Ju Jutsu instruction to, for instance, sport/point Karate groups and some haven't ever seen it or used it before because they are always fighting/sparring with semi contact mitts. Glove fighting limits the wide range of powerful open hand moves that are available to the self defence orientated practitioner.

How does the strike work? Well it can come from most angles and can be delivered powerfully.

The 'rising' palm heel comes from the hip. The striking hand well flexed back for maximum penetration on impact. It shoots up and slams under the chin or the philtrum (base of nose), finishing hand position is almost flexed back like a waiter will carry a tray of drinks. It fits naturally under the two targets mentioned and both carry KO potential.

The inverted palm heel is a close range strike like a boxers hook only the open heel hand smashes across the jaw powerfully, an unexpected and effective shot close up, especially in a vertical grapple.

Straight palm heel can be driven into the body, solar plexus and ribs being the main frontal targets, kidneys and the base of the skull being the rear ones.

Reverse or upside down palm heel hits the pubic bone or groin area, then the fingers can open, seize and rip the testicles. In some Kung Fu systems I believe this technique is called 'monkey steals the peaches' (a pretty apt description!)

Also the palm heel driven into the elbow joint of an extended limb can cause a weapon disarm, a dislocation or set up an armbar or lock.

The side palm heel whips up and into the jaw with a stiff arm. If you can get the proper body weight travelling with this blow it can be devastating. The ear drum is another possible target.

As a weapon to attack the head I feel it takes some beating, this comes from my own experiences. But don't take my word for it, go and experiment and use it. As said it is an overlooked but highly potent Atemi strike that is an essential part of any good self protection plan.

Chapter 8
'Two's company, Three's definitely a crowd!

'Handling multiple attackers.'

When most people begin their journey into martial arts, they probably have visions of obtaining those magical skills, where they will be able to dispatch assailant after assailant with relative ease, just like the film or video hero from the many martial arts epics!

Once they have journeyed a while they begin to realise that to achieve such things are nigh on impossible. Even with many years of hard training under their belts, if they are honest they will admit handling more than one attacker is very hard to do and come out unscathed. Others though that live in a fantasy world of martial arts will still profess how they can easily do it!

After all they have done it many times in the Dojo and on demonstration teams!
But lets just hold it a minute and go for a reality check here with these people, and ask a few vital questions.

Firstly, were the attacks rehearsed, i.e. did you know what was coming at you? Secondly, did the 'attackers' take it is turns to come in and deliver their attack? Thirdly, did they dutifully fall down after your first blow, sweep etc? If so, then this is not what multiple attack is all about. No doubt if you trained in the above methods it is great fun and you will develop your technique and reflexes, but it will not help you against a 'real' multiple attack scenario on the street, why?

Well you must remember if your multiple attack strategies stem from film/video, you must remember the stuntmen are getting paid good money to fall over for the 'star' of the film, also they must make him/her look their best!

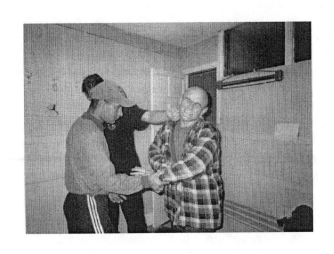

In reality your attackers will not be falling down for you. They will attempt to attack as a pack, all at once, or try to blind side you, then sucker punch you out. They will not line up in regimental order waiting for their turn to 'have a go', nor will they all circle you in fighting stance like one of the classic old time Kung Fu movies!

The attackers will be like a pack of wolves after a lamb. They will crowd, imitate, hurl abuse, push, shove and then attack in savage fury! If you are overwhelmed and go to the floor they will kick and stomp you to bits and they will not stop!

So is it an impossible situation you may ask? Answer, no, not impossible, just extremely difficult and dangerous.

In the 70's and early 80's 1 was exposed more than once to multiple attack scenarios in football crowds that were notorious for trouble back then (yes they have football teams here in Bristol....I think)! It is a frightening experience and one when you just want to run and hide, it is complete and utter mayhem! I have witnessed many horrific injuries in these situations and the pure blood lust of a mob of aggressive and violent people, these experiences made me closely examine multiple attack rituals (two or more people) and I have broken it down into three categories, these are just my own personal opinions.

No. 1 - Planned or pre-meditated attack. This comes from maybe trouble in your line of work (doormen, security, Police) where for one reason or another you have 'upset' person or persons who want to even things up. It can also happen in everyday life, depending on the type of life you lead. (*read Thugs, mugs and violence by Jamie O'Keefe*)

Anyway the bottom line is you are going to be set up as a victim of a planned multiple attack. It will be planned to the finest detail, when, where, how to catch you at your most vulnerable (i.e. after leaving a restaurant on an evening with your wife/girlfriend). It will come fast and ferocious with a cold edge of professionalism.

No. 2 - Spontaneous attack. Usually a mugging or rape situation, where it has suddenly been decided you look a likely candidate for the attack. It is not rehearsed, you are just in the wrong place at the wrong time! (*read Dogs don't know Kung fu by Jamie O'Keefe*).

No. 3 - Escalating attack. This being you have dealt with or are dealing with a solitary attacker when suddenly others join in either friends of the attacker or just interested parties who like a good 'tear up'. It is a sudden surprise to you and probably will come as a blindsided ambush type of attack.

How do you handle these situations? The big technique to help in all these scenarios is 'AWARENESS'. Without it you are in serious s**t!

In No 1 scenario, if you feel you may be a victim of a 'visit' then you must keep awareness at all times and not let your guard down for sometime, it could be weeks or months. Have some sort of 'equaliser' at hand, particularly at home for that unexpected call!

Make sure when you are out to be vigilant particularly of cruising cars. If you are aware and an ambush begins you will at least have the advantage of not being totally 'blown away' by surprise and will be able to react in some fashion (*flight or fight'*).

In No 2, being aware will help you protect your personal space. So if the muggers play is to try and mentally disarm you with the old 'have you got the time' or 'do you know the way to.. .' ploys you will have time to react. Use your hands to keep distance with innocent hand gestures but be ready to move. Don't let them get inside your hand distance or blind side you, move to your rear, keep alert.

No 3, If you are fighting the lone assailant in a crowded place and you finish them, gesture aggressively and shout at anyone else in the vicinity, something like 'does anybody else want some of this', you could at the same time be pinning your attacker with a knee or foot on the head or have them in a joint lock. What you are doing is verbally and visually diffusing a situation where someone else might want a go. Scan the area and watch for any movement and don't keep your guard down.

Awareness can help you survive!

It can literally stop you from being jumped on or surprised. But it is very hard to train it to be instinctive, you must work on it as much as any physical technique.
As for physical technique, you want to hit attackers in prime vital areas, eyes, throat, groin, chin/jaw, kneecaps. Use basic but powerful and targeted blows, nothing fancy or 'iffy'. Avoid grappling, throwing, joint locking, you will not have time, the more time you waste the more people you will be fighting. You need to be offensive and pre-emptive and explode with fury, go for the ring-leader usually the talker and then try and make an escape.
Remember there is no law that says you can't run! If you make an opening go for it unless your job dictates otherwise.

Remember, you don't have to wait to see your handy work, the order of the day is survival. So if you take one assailant out with a palm heel to the chin and another with a knifehand to the throat and a gap appears make for it!
As said before don't allow yourself to be crowded or closed down and don't allow yourself to be grabbed. No 3 scenario may find that happening if your awareness is down, someone may grab you from the rear. Then you need to know back head butts, elbows and stomps backed up with throws, if you go down with attacker to floor, strike him and get up quickly or use their body as a shield to ward off kicks or blows.

You need to train these scenarios in the Dojo and experience what it is like to have two or more people just pile into you!

You will find how mentally and physically demanding it is and how much conditioning you will need to absorb punishment if they get the drop on you. You will also need undying spirit to keep fighting and win the day. These are frightening demanding drills but they are 'real'.

Also try it against weapons and also you using weapons or makeshift items. Remember also if you get hold of a weapon from your attackers then use it as an 'equaliser' don't throw it away!

Don't forget, there is no easy solution, you will be fighting for your life, everything and anything will go. Getting a good rear choke or strangle on an attacker may buy you a little time to manoeuvre a getaway or use them as a shield.

If you want to stand any chance against more than one person you must drill these scenarios realistically but not as I mentioned at the start of this chapter like some martial arts 'demo', that will not help you.

There are no guarantees and you still might take a battering but at least you will have given it your best shot using sound tactics and techniques.

Also remember awareness is the big technique and a good pair of trainers for the getaway, good luck!

"Wild animals never kill for sport. Man is the only one whom the torture and death of his fellow human being is amusing in itself"

Chapter 9
All systems go!

'How our body reacts to violent confrontation'

The human body undergoes many chemical changes when in physical danger or in times of emotional stress. Depending on the circumstances the changes can vary in its degrees and the length of time they are sustained.

When we are in physical danger i.e. an impending victim of a violent encounter we will feel these bodily changes and put them down to fear. People who do not understand the chemical reactions within themselves and not know how to control them will immediately presume they are cowardly and these fear feelings are signs of weaknesses.

Everybody feels fear, from a mild 'butterflies' in the stomach, when you visit the dentist or doctor to a bigger build up when say taking your driving test or making a public speech to a mass build up when confronted by a violent situation, it is only natural, it is how you control the feelings that count. But to do this let's explore exactly what it is that is happening to us and maybe we can understand it better.

When under the immense stress that a violent encounter brings the body will prepare itself for 'fight' or 'flight', meaning it is getting ready for you to run or to go into 'combat mode' and defend yourself. Within the largest part of the brain the cerebrum lies the hypothalamus, this is a collection of specialised nerve centres which connect up with other important areas of the brain as well as the pitutary gland. It controls vital functions like eating, sleeping and temperature control as well as being linked to the endocrine (hormone) system. Under stress the hypothalamus working with the pituitary gland will signal the release of adrenaline from the adrenaline glands above the kidneys.

This substance rushes through the body at a great rate of knots producing a massive build up under dangerous conditions. It literally primes the body for action.

The face drains of colour, pupils dilate, mouth becomes dry, profuse sweating, voice is high pitched or quavering, blood pressure, heart and pulse rates increase. Stomach shuts down as blood supply is cut off with the blood going to heart and lungs for the sudden explosion of action that is going to happen. Surface blood vessels constrict as again supply is heading for vital organs.

You will find if you are cut there's not much bleeding on extremities like the limbs and if there is blood it will clot quickly. With the increase blood rush to heart/lungs you will be breathing rapidly and will have a job to control this. You may feel you need to empty your bladder or bowels. If looking down a barrel of a shotgun pointing at you, you might just do this!

With pupils dilating you will get tunnel vision, this is where your vision narrows down to the person in front of you who is causing you stress, this is when his mate will sneak in from the side and 'sucker punch' you! The most noticeable thing with the adrenaline build up will be shaking of the body and knees, sometimes this is extremely hard to control. The rule is not to let this build up go on too long but to make your decision for 'fight' or 'flight' as soon as possible. The longer you stall the harder it is to control the adrenaline build up. So you can see the feelings you may put down to 'pure fright' are natural. Adrenaline will give you a powerhouse feeling of increased strength and power for a short burst period.

Also worth noting that the liver will also secrete a substance called endorphin's into the blood stream these can be like an anaesthetic to deaden body pain whilst engaged in a fight and also produces white blood corpuscles to fight infection. Now if you choose to engage in defending yourself, when it kicks off, the bodies systems will come into play. The liver is the orchestra of the production of energy. It will store energy giving products like carbohydrates or glycogen then direct and release it to the necessary cells requiring it.

The energy system will start with a substance called adenosine triphosphate (ATP) the body must have a constant supply of this. When the body explodes in fast action like all out punching, kicking or grappling you will find by using the 'fast twitch' muscles, the anaerobic system (without oxygen), the first burst of ATP in this system will only last 4 to 5 seconds. Once the ATP is used up the body is left with a substance known as adenosine dephosphate (ADT) and another called creatine phosphate (CP) these combine to make a further supply of ATP which again will not last too long.

A third stage of energy can be achieved by lactic acid entering the blood stream and taken to the liver which will convert it into the bloodstream as glycogen and power the body once more. The only problem is all the lactic acid cannot be exchanged and builds up in the system when this happens exercise must cease because it cramps up the muscles. To overcome this you must reduce the level of exercise to allow the aerobic (with oxygen) system to take over. Once this happens the energy system process can start all over again.

The anaerobic system can be developed and improved by eating the proper diet and increasing B vitamin intake, as well as practising and extending explosive rapid exercise. Once over 40 years of age you will not be able to improve the fast twitch muscle that you have, it cannot be done.

To recap and put the energy in general terms, when involved in combat you will use both Anaerobic (fast twitch) and Aerobic (slow twitch) systems. When throwing a flurry of punches or kicks in rapid succession you will by using the anaerobic system, if you are held or pinning a person on the floor you will be using the aerobic system. If you want to develop as a martial artist, boxer, wrestler etc you will have to develop both systems due to the changes in combat. Also big build ups of adrenaline can make you one minute strong, the next very weak, be prepared for this. Obviously these systems are used in any sport as well. Sprinters rely on anaerobic work, marathon runners more aerobic. Different levels of fitness will determine how long you will last in the anaerobic system, but when involved in combat/fighting, guts, iron will, determination and unbreakable spirit are also factors, possibly the key factors. Read **Jamie O'Keefe's** book *'Pre-emptive strikes for winning fights'* to gain a clearer understanding of winning a fight in seconds within your anaerobic capabilities.

Going back to the adrenaline feelings. After a confrontation you will come down very fast from the high and may feel nausea, be sick, feel weak and sometimes depressed, this is the side effects of adrenaline.

Can you ever rid the body of the 'fear feelings' answer No you can't. But exposing yourself to the feelings of adrenaline regularly or now and again you can go a long way to reducing them somewhat.

If facing conflict breath deeply and strongly, push the adrenaline around the body, swallow try and get saliva in the mouth.

Control the voice, show no emotion on your face unless you want to, cover the shakes in your limbs by the way you stand or hold yourself and don't wait too long to decide your actions, once they start the feelings will escalate and you can get on with the job at hand.

Once you understand what's happened in your body when under extreme stress or threat, then you can find the best way for you to personally control it.

You should drill with a partner shouting, swearing and verbally insulting each other and get used to the emotional feelings this gives you. You will get an adrenal rush just from this. You may feel fearful angry, tongue-tied, embarrassed, whatever. Raw violent aggression in your face does this to you. It has 'froze' more people and beaten them long before a punch has been thrown.

This aspect of violence can be a psychological killer. If you don't deal with this type of thing it will hit you hard in a live situation and even if you are a good fighter it can throw you mentally off balance. I have known people with little or no fighting ability 'back down' another with just raw verbal aggression. In my childhood days I was the victim of this more times than I care to remember. Looking back the people who were verbally 'beating me up' were nothing and I probably could have beat them if it went to physical. But I didn't know how to handle the verbal threats and I wasn't confident enough in myself to have a try, I hate those memories. But I have learnt from them, I have seen examples of it many times after and I have fronted out people who later on in life tried the same tricks.

You must learn to get rid of your 'hot spots'. Meaning if being called a 'fat bastard', 'four eyed bastard', bald bastard etc, hurts you and gets you 'foaming at the mouth' you are in trouble because your antagonist is mentally controlling you. He knows what 'winds' you up and will forever push the right button.

By doing the verbal drills you will gradually get rid of 'your hot spots' and in the end the verbal will run like water off a 'ducks back'. Practice it and don't under-estimate it otherwise you will be fighting all the time and either eventually end up doing a stretch or end up on a slab.

Understand your mind then use it as a major weapon for defence!

"Our minds are lazier than our bodies"

Chapter 10
Impact Ju Jutsu

'Hard core training for Combat'

In these times of increasing realism in the Martial Arts most practitioners are finding the need for some sort of impact and contact training. Training to punch, strike or kick fresh air or touch striking is just not enough to really know if your technique will stand up under pressure when the moment of truth arrives.

Of course some have known the need for impact training for years, others are only just discovering it's values now.

In the system of Ju Jutsu (Kempo Goshin Jutsu) I have been training and teaching impact training for some years. Unique in some ways as most Ju Jutsu systems in general don't really practise, say, bag work, focus pads, etc, although some may have changed their ways in recent times.

One of my early instructors, Shihan Mick Upham, was a great believer in impact training and also contact training, his Ju Jutsu was real and he wanted to make sure it worked. He passed this idea on to me when at the time most Ju Jutsu training was very defensive based block, strike, throw, lock self defence techniques. He was the first to show me offensive Ju Jutsu and also working Ju Jutsu against a gloved up opponent just coming at you with any punches or kicks. This was all very new and revolutionary in the early 80's. I have carried on and developed these ideas and still teach these concepts today. Now of course everybody is beginning to cross train in these ideas.

I can remember being on a course with Shihan Upham and a few others from the Ju Jutsu systems, training with members of the Israeli Anti-terrorist squad participating in no holds barred fighting, anything goes, as long back as the 80's.

Testing Ju Jutsu skills under extreme pressure hoping you can come out in one piece! This type of training was not new to us then, but only recently have others begun to see the value of this type of practise. From my own observations of this type of practise you need equal amounts of striking and grappling knowledge, good physical conditioning and tremendous spirit!

Only regular impact/contact training can give you this, without it you will never know exactly what you are capable of doing when the s**t hits the fan!

Every martial artist feels they are able to defend themselves and usually envisage themselves as some sort of un-stoppable fighting machine!

When you have performed for an hour on pad work and you feel sick to your stomach, legs feel like liquorice and your arms are like lead and you find yourself next up against an opponent whaling away at you with the gloves on, or trying to choke you out in a ground grapple, then you can really analyse your fighting capacity.

You will be greatly surprised, shocked or even disappointed. This is what Geoff Thompson's been doing in his Animal Day sessions and what he has been teaching in his seminars, yet some still choose to ignore it, prepared to keep on believing that when it goes down they'll be OK and their training will stand up to it!

I personally state unless you do some sort of contact and impact training and try and reach for some realism you will fall sadly short of the mark in a real street situation.

It's not an easy step to take, no one relishes the thought of being battered about but with safe monitoring and being exposed to gradually increasing degrees of contact, anyone can do it.

Each month in my Ju Jutsu classes 1 will do an impact training session where we will work punching and striking the focus pads, kicking the shields, continuous throwing drills, gloved fighting, ground fighting, not just grappling but one person gloved and punching the other just grappling. Upright striking and grappling, closing a gap and clinching against all out punching.

Punching pads in mounted, guard, side positions and from on the knees, two on to one all out sparring and heavy conditioning work for stamina and body toughening, etc etc.

These sessions are physically and mentally draining but people keep coming back because they realise the need for them. I have seen people come out of themselves and change. It has increased their confidence and abilities no end, they know they have pushed themselves above and beyond what they thought they were capable of and found that hidden bit of extra. When the sessions are over and you have recovered you feel great, alive and a sense of achievement. You can only get this going through adversity in any shape or form. I have only the utmost respect for those who take on this form of training.

Any Martial Art can supplement impact/contact training into their practise with a little imagination and 1'm sure they will feel the benefits. You don't have to sacrifice any other part of the art you are practising, just add to it, if this sort of thing appeals.

More details of this type of training can be found on my videos, Impact Ju Jutsu Vol's. 1, 2 and 3.

Ordering information for these videos are at the end of this book.

> *"The bottom line in Self Defence is*
> *learn to hit F*****g hard!"*

Geoff Thompson (Who can)

Chapter 11
'Getting to the point'

'Tactics and techniques against a knife'

Billy said goodbye to his friends, it had been a good night out, the film had been good, the pizza afterwards even better, they had all promised to do it again soon. Billy started off down the road, his mind pre-occupied with the thoughts of the evening when suddenly, as he passed a shop doorway, a hand snaked out, grabbed him roughly by the collar and pulled him into the doorway. Billy was slammed against the shuttered doors and then for the first time he saw his attacker, but he also saw the blade of the knife rammed up under his chin. He froze, panic setting in. His thoughts whirled around in his head. 'Why hadn't he been more aware?' What does this person want?' Will he cut me, stab me? Suddenly his train of thought was broken by a snarling whisper from his attacker. *'Shut up, don't move and listen, your money now or I'll cut you badly, man, money now!'* Billy knew he was in big trouble.....

The above scenario was made up for this chapter, but the threat of mugging at knife-point isn't a fantasy. Maybe it's happened to you, a member of your family, a friend? You constantly read about this type of mugging in the newspapers or hear about it on the news.

Unfortunately many people, young and old alike, have found themselves confronted by a mugger armed with a blade demanding money, valuables or sometimes with more sinister motives.

What can you do in this situation? Do you give up your valuables? Do you fight back? Will you risk being hurt? Is it possible to disarm your assailant? What should I know? What should I do?

Questions hopefully this chapter can answer for you.

First of all let's examine the manner of attack. You are held at knife-point. This means the attacker hasn't made their mind up yet whether to actually use the blade against you, or they may not wish to use it at all. They are making the knife a psychological threat. They feel the presence of it pushed against your body will be enough to make you succumb to their demands. Usually they are carrying the knife and brandishing it to make up for their below par fighting abilities unarmed and to give them a psychological boost, a confidence giver.

They may be an out and out coward below the rough front, but it is still an extremely dodgy job finding out. As I said, they may not intend to actually use the knife, but sudden changing circumstances or sheer desperation may force their hand, an example being a junkie looking for money for a fix, a very unpredictable assailant.

Next, how important are your valuables to you? In a lot of self defence courses, books, etc, they recommend giving up your wallet, handbag, purse. They're not as important as your life. That is good, sound and sensible advice. The average person may accept this and give up the said mentioned articles. But others of you may not. You may be furious that some 'low life' wants to relieve you of your hard earned money. Money you worked for, money for your family, kids, mortgage, holiday etc. Why the hell should you give it up, you may say! A fair point and one that isn't easy to answer. Each individual will have their own thoughts on this matter, it is a personal thing.

One solution to this dilemma is to carry on you a 'dummy' purse or wallet with a few pounds in it. When asked for your money draw out the false one and throw it at the muggers feet then run.

By the time they realise they have nothing you will be long gone.

This technique is outlined in more detail in the excellent book *'Dogs don't know Kung Fu'* by my friend and colleague **Jamie O'Keefe.**

But sometimes you may not have this choice or if it is your car keys they want or your jewellery, shopping etc. At the end of the day it will be your choice which you do.

I can't advise that, the only thing I can say is you must know what you are doing, especially if a knife is involved, one mistake could be fatal. But again you can't really know how you will react until that moment of truth. If you go with the advice of give up your money, wallet, etc, what if the attacker demands your wedding ring, the gold necklace you had bought for your wedding anniversary? Some people will put their lives before such items, right or wrong? Your choice.

So now we come to the big question, what if I decide to defend myself? Alright the bottom line is even a skilled martial artist or combat veteran will still have problems defending against weapons.

It is a skill you must practice daily to have a chance. A 12 year old youth with a knife is every bit as dangerous as a full grown adult assailant. Don't underestimate anyone armed! One thing going for you is that the knife is static, meaning the attacker is not trying to stab, slash, rip or cut you with it, a much more difficult and frightening prospect. At least in this instance you know where the blade is and because they haven't instantly stabbed you with it, indicates a good chance they may not want to, but just use the knife's presence as a threat. So what do you need to know, if you decide to put up a fight?

Firstly no sudden quick movements, give nothing that will panic the attacker and cause them to cut you. Remember this person could have been hanging around for some time waiting for a suitable target.

Remember also they have got to be desperate to do this in the first place. They will be 'hyped' up on adrenaline, nervous, twitchy, not knowing exactly what will happen in those first moments of confrontation. In their own way they will be as frightened as yourself. If they are 'drug users' they may well be totally 'strung out' and highly unpredictable, any sudden move on your part may be a fatal mistake.

So in those opening seconds be totally compliant, give them no course to think you could be a threat. Raise your hands up in surrender, say something like 'OK you can have the money, you're the boss, I'm not going to mess with you!'

Anything along those lines to relax them somewhat. To bring their adrenaline down, to bring their guard down. Just do what ever they say and be totally compliant.

If you are a more mature, or elderly person saying something like 'Alright, give me a moment I've just come out of hospital last week after having a serious operation, let me get my breath back', may work well to mentally disarm the attacker or actually feign a heart attack (if you are a good actor), to buy yourself time. Whatever it takes to mentally drop the assailants guard and take his mind off the weapon. Even if they say 'do you think I'm going to fall for that, means their mind is not 100% on the knife'.

Don't say things like 'Got to have a knife to feel brave, eh?' or 'Put the knife down and let's see how tough you are?' These things may only serve to 'wind' them up and they may cut you in anger and frustration.

Remember play it 'cool' don't give nothing away in your words or actions until the time is right.

The following are suggested methods based on training and working with people that have had to use them in 'live' situations, i.e. special forces, bodyguards, security, doormen, etc. They have worked under stress conditions, others of you out there may have your own methods, as long as you understand the psychological aspects of disarming then you will have a good chance. For those of you with **NO** training experience then I am not suggesting you just go out and attempt to disarm a knife wielding assailant, that would be suicide, but I suggest you look at some martial arts/self protection training that can give you this aspect. The suggested techniques here may give you some pointers. Lastly remember you may get cut during the defences.

You must learn to carry on to the finish. Whatever happens, once you begin there is no turning back.

We'll take the scenario that you are forced up against a wall, the knife is pressed to the side of your neck. You defensively bring your hands up in a 'surrender' fashion and do the dialogue previously outlined. When the opponent is distracted suddenly whip your hand inside the attackers knife arm and knock it up and away from your neck then grab the knife wrist as you simultaneously drive a claw finger strike into their eyes, now follow up with a knee to the groin and spin them around into the wall. If they still have the knife in their hand, press their knife arm against the wall and smash a few hard punches into their inner bicep, hitting the brachial artery, sandwiching it against the wall, this will paralyse the arm forcing the knife to drop, a follow-up knee to solar plexus, claw grab to throat or heel palm to chin should end the confrontation!

Using the wall to disarm is a great move and often overlooked unless you train for 'real life' scenarios and not dojo ones!

If you are again held up with a knife to the outer side of the neck and you get outside it with a parry, you can slip a knee into the ribs then drive your attacker by the back of the neck head first into the wall. A follow up knee to the base of the spine will set up a disarm.

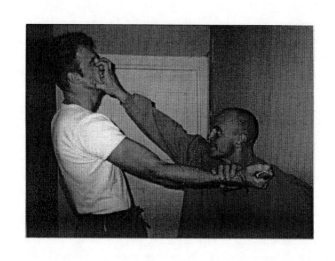

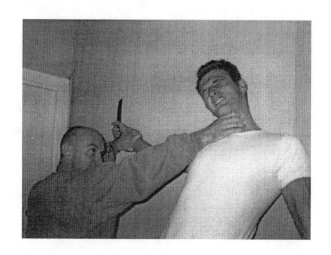

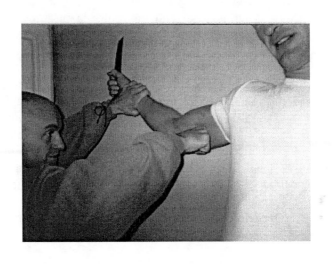

This time press knife arm against wall and smash your forearm into the elbow joint, once again sandwiching and crippling the joint between your forearm and the wall, an instant disarm. Pulling them backward and kicking away the hock of the knee will bring them down for a finish with a kick or stomp.

What if the blade is pushed into the stomach and you are told to freeze so your hands are down by your side? Again mentally disarm, this time they will be a lot closer to you. Suddenly bring your hands up to their knife wrist, grab and turn your body sideways away from direct path of knife. This should bring their body weight forward quickly towards the wall. Ram their knifehand into brickwork and rub violently their knuckles up and down the wall for a release.

If you clamp their straightened elbow under your armpit from there you will be able to dislocate it with an 'elbow crush' to finish.

These are just a few examples, by NO means all you can do.

Whatever you decide you must do it quickly and sharply, control the knife arm, go in whole heartily to vital points, get it done quickly.

Remember it's a close up confrontation, if you don't practice at this range you will have problems. If you are up against a large assailant and a powerful one don't mess about, go for vital points. Once you have deflected the blade don't overlook kneeing or grabbing testicles to bring their head down, butting the face, elbowing the throat or jaw and hitting the knife arm/hand or anywhere else. Also close up as a distraction move in the opening seconds, spitting into opponents eyes/face will instantly make them 'cringe', then go for your counter.

Wristlock/armlocks are too risky in a knife defence unless you are very highly skilled. The average person is better off smashing the joint or dislocating it, rather than trying to subdue the assailant with a hold or lock. If it is messed up you may not get a second chance because now you are faced with a moving knife attack.

If you feel you couldn't fight back remember the motive may not be robbery but assault or rape which in that case you have no choice!

When you have distance between yourself and an armed assailant i.e. Five foot or more, then run, look for an exit and escape. Why stand in a fancy Martial Arts stance, flash your dan grade license and hope he will turn to 'quivering jelly!'. This is how you see most knife defences performed in magazines etc. This is the 'macho' conditioning process that Martial Arts have given certain people and they really believe they are invincible. This is rubbish! Martial Arts have 'sold' people a very dangerous and totally irresponsible attitude towards weapons.

If you want to get good advice about dealing with knives and other edged weapons I suggest you get *'Old school-New school'* **by Jamie O'Keefe** to see how he advises bouncers to deal with knife attacks. After all, bouncers must get in more confrontations than any other profession than I can think of.

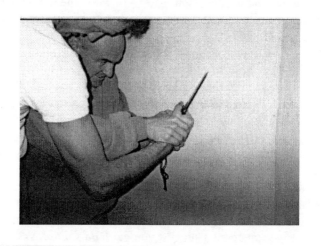

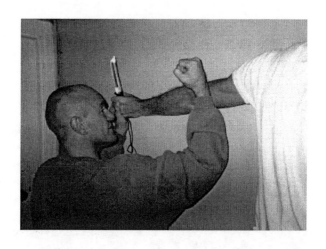

If you have four feet of distance or less and the attacker is brandishing a blade then start talking trying to mentally disarm him at the same time trying to increase your distance and look for a possible makeshift weapon as an equaliser.

If you are in a job (security) which requires you to approach somebody at this range that you suspect may have a weapon then 'switch' on and scan their hands. If one is hidden from view demand to see their hands. Blow their element of a surprise attack out of the water, let them know, you know they are 'carrying'. They will eventually have to show their hands armed or not, this ploy works well.

Any less distance than four feet and you will have to be fighting back.

It means for whatever reason you have dropped your guard and your assailant has caught you unawares. If the attacker is actually going to attack then you will have NO choice but to fight, this is a last resort. Expect to get cut, but you will have to be mentally strong and keep going. Attack the eyes and throat, try and get hold of the knife arm and pound your assailant with a barrage of strikes until they drop to the floor. Kick away the knife or pick it up if it is free. Never rush in to try and take it out of attackers hand if they are on the floor or if their fallen body has concealed it, just incase he is waiting for you.

If your job doesn't require it, the only time you would 'face off' a knife brandishing assailant is if you are protecting and shielding your family or loved ones or if you have absolutely no escape route and you know you will have to fight. In this case be aggressive, try and 'psyche' your attacker out, try to show no fear as if you have done this a 1000 times before. Smile grimly and beckon them in saying something like *'OK, give it your best shot, cause it's gonna be your last!'* If you have time get hold of a makeshift weapon, depending on your environment. Use a briefcase, dustbin lid as a shield, your coat, belt whatever. This all depends of course on time and your awareness.

Things to remember is that most muggers will not use a knife on you unless you do something stupid to force this.

People that 'show' knives are not usually the ones to use them, simply because if they wanted to they could have stabbed you and took your money to start with, they are being polite and asking you for it, under the threat of the knife!

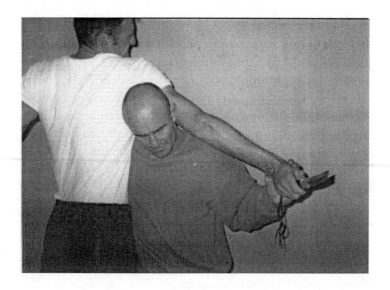

People that will use a blade will probably not let you see it until it is hurtling towards your body. This is where your awareness and distancing is of prime importance.

Sometimes you will see the knife. Particularly in crimes of passion or domestic disputes when one of the parties involved will 'snap' and pick up a knife and rush at the other person in a wild frenzy. This is probably the only time you would see the 'classic' ice pick over the head stab attack or the Norman Bates special as I like to refer to it! This form of attack is not common on the streets, it is usually slashes or stabs. Of course in a social environment glasses and bottles are slashing and stabbing implements to, as are screwdrivers, these normally are used in a panic type of attack by a would be car thief who is using the screwdriver to open a door or steal a radio and has been surprised by maybe the cars owner or the police.

Understanding weapons, their uses, strengths and weaknesses and how people will use them is essential, if you want to survive an encounter against them. Remember it is not impossible to defend and beat a knife attack but it requires great mental and physical ability, something's you must train realistically on a regular basis to hope to come out on top.

List of Life saving tips

1. Never underestimate anybody armed with a knife regardless of their size, age, or sex!
2. If engaged with a blade, expect to get cut....then fight on.
3. Never be macho or stupid, If you can escape, do so.
4. No amount of martial arts training can give you 100% success against a blade.
5. The best knife defence is awareness and avoidance.
6. Don't grapple or attempt to lock/restrain a knife attacker, it can be fatal.
7. Don't try to kick a knife from an assailants hand.
8. If somebody aggressively approaches you, watch their hands.
9. Don't attempt the classical 'X' block or rising block against a downward stab. It will not stop the blade penetrating you.
10. Get into the frame of mind that anybody who offers you violence, could be armed.

Chapter 12
'AMBUSH'
'The sneak attack'

The priority of a good self protection plan is awareness. Being alert and 'switched on' is essential to your street survival plan. By using awareness you will have the opportunity to spot, evaluate and take action (fight or flight) when a potentially dangerous or violent situation is encountered.

Of course sometimes we will make mistakes, after all we are only human and drop our safety antenna and that's when we can 'fall foul' to the ambush or sneak attack coming from the rear of you.

This sneak attack is a cowardly means of fighting but also extremely effective. Ladies are particularly vulnerable to this 'ambush' tactic and many recorded cases of assault, mugging and rape have stemmed from them being grabbed from the rear. Of course anybody can fall victim particularly if they are 'switched off' or distracted or pre-occupied.

In our busy everyday lives we are all guilty at times of walking around with our thoughts elsewhere and it takes a high degree of constant training to keep focused on our surroundings and the people in them.

If you are aware it is virtually impossible to be caught by surprise, especially with a 'sneak attack', but in some circumstances for whatever reason you may get caught and then you will have to defend yourself and know exactly what to do.

Learning to defend against rear grabs and holds must be in your repertoire of defensive tactics.

This chapter hopefully is going to look at some progressive ways of learning to counter the 'sneak' attack.

Firstly remember if an ambush attack is down to you lacking awareness then it will come in the form of a great shock to you and you will experience that momentary 'freeze' syndrome or as Geoff Thompson refers to it, 'Adrenaline dump'. This is where you will get the lead weight feeling in the pit of your belly and the legs will go a little jelly like.

If 'Switched off'
The rear attack can come as a big surprise

This moment and how you react to it will determine the outcome of the situation.

A lot of people who have been victims of a rear sneak attack have frozen terribly and have not been able to fight back at all. I believe training to react as quickly as possible to the attack is the prime factor for survival. It is being able to get the brain to swiftly realise what is happening and then trigger a message to the body to react.

In training we can run into a problem. How can we 'simulate' that surprise feeling, after all if we are drilling this type of technique we will know the attack is coming and be pre-warned, and the senses will be on red alert ready for the coming assault, this is not a realistic portrayal of what we are looking for. So how can we overcome this and apply pressure and realism.

Firstly we have got to learn the motor skills of some basic, but effective counter techniques to a variety of rear attacks. In the early stages nothing too complex that requires great thought and fine intricate skills.

For example against a rear body hold with the arms pinned respond with a foot stomp, rear head butt and a hard rear thrust with your backside.

Simple but effective. If it's a rear choke, go for a testicle squeeze, bite into the choking arm and shoot a rear elbow into the solar plexus.

Work through all rear grabs and holds in this manner. Other rear attacks can be strangles, hair grabs, full nelson, wrist grabs, arm grabs, etc. More advanced attacks can be knife hold ups from rear and garrotting type moves.

Once you have your response to a certain hold then gradually speed up the attack and the intensity, increasing the pressure.

Next stage is use the delayed attack drill. Get your partner to turn their back and then delay attacking for say 5 seconds, then 10 then 20 and so on, mix it up. The partner will not then become robotic in their practise, it will bring an element of uncertainty into the training.

Joint break to escape rear strangle

Biting can gain you a release from a chokehold

The back elbow- an effective counter-move!

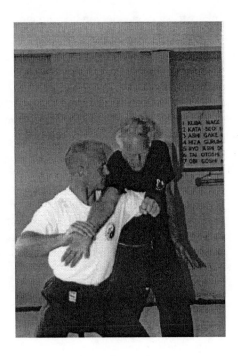

Next step, get your partner to shut their eyes. Now no outside stimulation can interfere and not being able to see adds an element of unknown to the drill. When you attack, your partner will experience a 'jump' sensation to their bodies and a touch of the 'Adrenaline Dump' we mentioned earlier.

These drills can be done with one particular grab until it becomes instinctive. Then the next stage can have your partner waiting and you can come in hard and fast with any rear hold and they have to instantly react.

This is the advanced stage and will definitely pressure you.

Also you can put one person in a circle or get them to walk past a line of people and one will jump out and rear grab them without prior notice, these drills also test the reaction time to the attack, whi.ch remember is the 'key factor'.

Be careful, particularly with rear chokes or garrotting techniques, have some degree of control because the windpipe is easy to damage.

Another method is to get one person to engage another in a frontal verbal scenario. For example asking him the time or directions, then get another person to blind-side him and attack from the back. This also works well to test reactions.

As I said the actual techniques you choose are not important as long as you can make them work. If you're into grappling you may find it easy to throw someone over with a shoulder throw, body drop, winding throw etc.

If you prefer striking use rear head butt, foot stomp, back elbow, groin grabs etc. As long as it works then that's fine.

If you don't want to be a victim of an ambush then when you are out and about stay 'tuned in'.

Vulnerable times are entering and exiting vehicles, in and out of lifts, garden paths, entering your home building etc. These are times when you can get caught, be aware of this and try to eliminate these dangers.

Also don't neglect training against the 'sneak attack', it must be addressed because if you don't and the situation arises it will be a frightening and extremely dangerous encounter.

Look out for further details on this subject like in my previous book, *'I Thought you'd be bigger.'*

Throw counter to a full nelson hold

The victim takes charge of the attacker

Chapter 13
Visual Scanning to avoid Ambush attacks

We have dealt in the previous chapters with what to do when trouble erupts in front of you and you have no other choice than to physically fight back, this as always is your last option. Being aware can cut down the chances of becoming a victim of violence by about 70% I would say.

This day and age everybody seems to be busy, pre-occupied by other things and are just switched off when out and about on the streets.

Most of the time they will put themselves in situations of danger from their own making and then wonder why it happened to them.   You can bet your life anybody who has survived a mugging for instance will say after the event, 'I just didn't see them,' or 'They came out of nowhere'.

Although it may seem like this to the victim, it is never the case. Some muggers will have located their target and followed them for some distance before initiating their assault. There is always some sort of pre-planning. It all depends how switched on you are to what is happening around you.

Here's an example, story of two soldiers separately tracking through enemy countryside. One comes to the edge of a field and sees across the other side a farmhouse, he is cold and hungry and is seeking shelter, so he lets those feelings over come natural caution and opens the gate into the field and begins walking across it. A few steps in he notices a sign post face down in the mud but walks on over it in his eagerness to reach shelter, two steps on he is blown to bits by a hidden land mine! Later the other soldier reaches the same field, he also is cold, tired and hungry, he to sees the farm house and goes through the gateway into the field, as he passes the sign post on the ground he hesitates and reaches down and picks it up, on the face side it reads 'Danger Minefield'! He quickly leaves the field, still tired and hungry but very much alive!

People in this day and age are walking into the proverbial 'minefield' all the time and have no idea at all that they are doing it!

When writing this book a tragic death occurred in my hometown of Bristol. It was the shocking murder of a young lady, which deemed nation-wide coverage. These terrible events seem to be happening on a far too regular basis today, but when it happens on your 'doorstep' so to speak it really hits home and makes you 'sit up' and take notice.

Through reading the facts of what happened the young lady appears to have made one fatal mistake, that unknowingly cost her life. She left a local night-club in the early hours of the morning after borrowing £5 from her brother for a taxi, but then it is alleged that for reasons unknown she decided to walk the few miles journey home. Along that route home she meet her murderer. If she had taken the taxi, would she be alive today? Probably yes. Regrettable she allegedly chose to risk the walk. How many more of us can say we have done the same thing, took the gamble to walk home late at night, or go for that short cut over the 'playing fields', except that lift from the guy who works in your office? It can be a costly gamble, can you see it's just going into that minefield.

Maybe that soldier could have avoided the mines if he thread carefully, it would be a risk, a gamble but he might just do it once. But twice or three times that's asking a lot. But of course in my little story he didn't even know it was a minefield in that case he had no chance.

Now think about that for a moment, people take that gamble every day with their safety or others don't even acknowledge it's a gamble.

To stop yourself ever being in a situation where you suddenly think 'shit' I don't want to be here, you must start to heighten your awareness, use your visual skills to scan your environment and the people in it, give yourself a chance to at the very least be able to prepare for an attack. It's like a sprinter who doesn't get on his 'blocks' on time or a horse that will not stay on the line before a race.

When the 'starter' goes they are on their back foot and very rarely recover the lost impetus.

Judgement can be clouded sometimes especially where alcohol is concerned. I have known people totally rational without it, but then take extreme uncharacteristic risks under it's influence. When your judgement is clouded your awareness levels will drop to non existent, that's why so much violence is associated with alcohol, because some people just don't see the trouble until it has erupted in their faces.

This is why clubs and pubs employ door supervisors, if they are good they can 'sniff' out potential trouble well before it kicks off and prevent it getting worse.

You will have to cultivate the same awareness and scanning abilities in your own personal everyday life, not easy but it can be done.

Here is a little exercise you can do to heighten your levels of awareness. When you go to work, whether you drive, take public transport or walk the same route everyday, visually pay attention to your surroundings. I guarantee something will be different on that route every day but because familiar to us we no longer really look. This is the 'looking without seeing' concept that Peter Consterdine talks about in the excellent 'Streetwise' book.

Now if you had to go to a new place of work, you would be fully receptive to landmarks, places and people because you want to get to know that route. The old saying 'familiarity breeds contempt' holds true. When we grow familiar with something we take it for granted and 'switch off'. So if every weekend you walk home from a club and not bother with a lift, you begin to feel OK about it. It's familiar, nothing will happen. Well, there is that stretch of dark road with the street lamps out but 1 expect they'll be on this week, anyway it was all right the last 2 weeks, so it's bound to be all right this time.........isn't it?

Here is another tale about familiarity. Years back I worked as a foreman in a timber yard and I used to get into work early some mornings to sort things out for the day.

Also sometimes a member of staff would come in to open up the main showroom. Now one day I was coming through the gate the same time as a colleague, he was on his way to open the showroom. This guy in his spare time was a sergeant in the T.A. and had been known to still think he was in the army whilst at work! This morning on the spur of the moment I thought I would have a bit of fun with him! I waited until he opened the showroom doors. I knew as always he would have to go to a cupboard by the far side of the showroom to switch on the electricity to light the place up. I quietly followed him in through the door and came across him bent over in this cupboard looking for the power switch. I came up behind him, put my fingers in his back and shouted 'give us the f.....g money now and don't piss me about'. He fell to his knees with hands held up in surrender, his face turning the colour of milk, stammering 'alright'. He then turned to face me and recognition began to dawn on him. 'You bastard' he croaked, 'You nearly gave me a heart attack!' I couldn't stop laughing, that army training really kicked in at the moment of truth!!

Apart from the funny story it showed that he had got familiar with a routine and had let his awareness drop to zero. That scenario could have been real.

If you are out on the streets be observant. For instance no one should come up behind you and over take you whilst walking and make you 'jump'. You should know if there is somebody walking behind you or across the street from you. If you are on your own at night then stay alert and know their every move. Sometimes it can be perfectly innocent and it's just somebody on their way home like you, but then again it could be somebody with more sinister motives.

If you are aware you can then evaluate the situation and make a decision on what to do 'flight or fight.' If you are not switched on the decision will be made for you!

Take this example:- You are walking along the street and about 200 yards up the road you see a group of youths they are rowdy, they have been drinking but as they see you they become quieter and huddle together whispering and glancing your way.

You are switched on and have seen all this. You decide there and then to cross the road and go up the main street, it will mean 10 minutes longer walk but it will keep you in a more populated and well lit area. You take this action and arrive home safe.

Example 2:- You are hurrying home, it's cold, you are longing for a hot bath, a nice meal and an evening in front of the telly. As you walk up the street you see the gang of youths but you don't really register any danger, you have had a long day at work and just want to get home.
As you pass the gang one steps out in front of you and says 'going somewhere?', as the others close in...........

You see by those 2 examples how your original awareness can effect the outcome of the scenarios. We are back again to the minefield story.
Visual scanning can become instinctive with training, but as with anything worthwhile in life you will have to work on it.
It doesn't mean you become paranoid about everything and everyone, but just begin to work on heightening your basic survival instincts.
You all work on survival instincts everyday, like when crossing a road you look for traffic, driving you obey the traffic signals (well almost). By doing these things subconsciously you think nothing of them, they have been inbred in you for many years. Yet people can do something crazy like hitch hike and take a lift from a stranger without concern.
Here's another example. How many of you have a security chain on your front door? How many of you use it ALL the time? How many of you use it at night, but freely open your door in the daytime? You see habits and rituals can lead to trouble.
Again awareness in and around your house can go a long way to preventing trouble. If you see a car parked outside or across the road for some length of time with a couple of men sat in it, is it totally innocent and to be dismissed or is it worth jotting down the registration, make and colour of car just incase.

Paranoid? or good awareness? It's down to you.

If you like to go out on the town and go to clubs etc then a little fore thought can prevent danger. If a club or pub is known for constant trouble and violence then don't go there, there are plenty more around to choose from. Yet I have heard people say, '1 can't believe it, every Saturday 1 go into that club there's trouble, it really pisses me off!' Then why go there?

If you do frequent such places then you must be prepared for the consequences. It's like saying everytime I walk up that street this dog runs out of a garden and chases me, what do I do? Answer, go up another street. Avoidance is better than confrontation if it can be used. I would rather view the animals in the zoo from the recommended safe distance and not be in the cage with them!

Having to get physical is the last line of a good self protection programme. I personally would like to exhaust all other options first before I got to that one. I can handle this option, I have trained most of my life for it but I will still choose primarily not to be there in the first place and want to be in control of my choice and not let somebody else control my options for me. This is extremely important.

No amount of training can guarantee results when it gets physical, it can only lower the odds. As my good mate and fellow self protection teacher Jamie O'Keefe will say, *'Anybody can do anybody, you just have to find a way*!' and how right he is!

So start getting a good awareness programme under way, and as I tell my children when they say to me 'Dad the kid next to me in class keeps talking to me and I'm going to get in trouble, what can I do?'

My reply is "Move away from them, so when trouble comes you won't be involved."

Visual Scanning – Can you see the knife?

Appendices

In this book I dealt with mainly what to do when trouble had erupted and you have no option but to fight back. This is the last resort method of the whole self protection jigsaw.   There is much more involved in the complete plan.

To learn about prevention, awareness, evaluation and a whole host of topics read the excellent book **'Streetwise' by Peter Consterdine**, a complete bible of self protection.

To learn more about the type of assailants on the streets today, attack rituals, controlling etc read **Geoff Thompson's** classic text **'Dead or alive'.**

Ladies if you want to know about the realities of female self protection or you teach female self protection, you must read **'Dogs don't know Kung Fu'**. A guide to female self protection by **Jamie 0'Keefe.**

For information on knife attacks and how to deal with them check out **Pat O'Malleys** book **'At the sharp end'.**

Lastly if you are a small person who feels they cannot defend themselves with physical technique, then read my first book **'I thought you'd be bigger,' a** small persons guide to fighting back.

All these books can give you a complete guide to self protection. But as I said before reading, is not enough, you must absorb the information and make it part of your everyday life and also you must train the physical skills regularly.

A finishing shot

Throughout this whole book I have tried to impress on you that when trouble starts it will be up close. If you are not 'switched on' or don't practice your awareness then attack will always be unexpected and 'in your face'. When this happens you will have no choice left but to fight back and when you do you must give it everything you have got. You must be mentally ruthless and determined to win and survive. It will be a frightening situation but one you must come to terms with quickly or you will lose.

Sometime ago a gentleman gave me a call and asked if I would give him some self defence training. He said he had recently been the victim of an un-provoked assault on the streets of his hometown in broad daylight. He went on to tell me how he had been mentally shocked by it and how it had suddenly happened.

He told me that he had been doing some shopping in the city centre and as he was walking along the busy high street, he passed a shop doorway where three youths were standing. As he passed one of them said something to him, but he didn't catch what it was and just kept on walking. Suddenly one of the youths ran up and jumped in front of him, the other two in tow. The youths blocked his way saying *"C'mon then, you want a f- u - k—g fight do you? C'mon."*

The guy said later to me he was totally surprised and shocked at this 'person' shouting aggressively in his face. Before he could gather his senses the youth punched him in the head/kicking him to the pavement and then they all ran off. (Brave boys)

The victim had to go to the hospital for treatment for minor cuts and shock, it could have been worse. The thing he kept saying to me when we met was how totally surprised he was that it happened out of nothing in broad daylight. I had to first re-educate him on today's violence and it's perpetrators before we went any further.

Now he knows better, violence can happen anywhere, anytime!

As I have mentioned before unless you train in close quarter scenarios and technique you will find yourself sadly lacking when trouble comes knocking on your door.

So train hard and be safe. As always being aware and being able to avoid violence should be your priority but when you can't, hopefully the tactics outlined in this book will help.

TAKE CARE.

Kevin 0'Hagan 1998

Kevin 0'Hagan
23 Chester Road
St.George
Bristol
BS5 7AX

The End…..

Adverts

Will the reader please note that the following advertising section of the book is included to let you know of other Self Protection related merchandise.

You the reader, have not been charged for the printing or paper used in this section. The cost for this has been absorbed by New Breed Publishing.

The price that you have paid for this publication is for the knowledge, information and advice given by Kevin O'Hagan throughout the rest of this book.

Thank you

Ricky O'Keefe

Web Site

www.newbreedbooks.co.uk

IMPACT JUJUTSU Vol 1

**If you are serious about improving your
All round fighting skills and conditioning,
Then this video is for you.**

**Learn '*Secret*' skills for better striking,
Throwing and grappling
Plus many unique fitness and conditioning drills!**

"FISTFUL OF DYNAMITE"

**Yawara-Bo is an excellent and compact little weapon
That can be an instant source of painful control.**

**Anybody of any age can learn how to use this
Lethal little stick, quickly with good effect!**

BRISTOL GOSHIN JUTSU
COMBAT ACADEMY
PRESENTS

NEW VIDEO RELEASES

Featuring Kevin O'Hagan 6thDan

"FISTFUL OF DYNAMITE"
YAWARA-BO TECHNIQUES

60 mins of dynamic techniques using this small but
highly effective weapon...plus substitute makeshift
Yawara-bo's from everyday articles...!

Excellent value at **£14.00**

(*Please add £1.00 for postage and packing*)

Please make cheques payable to "**Kevin O'Hagan**"
and post to
23 Chester road, St.George, Bristol BS5 7AX

Genuine 60 minutes of action guaranteed

'Down & Out'

**Grappling and groundwork is the 'In thing'
Within Martial arts at present.**

**If you want to expand your knowledge within this area,
this video is for you.**

**It's loaded with basic and advanced
throws and takedowns, with a
Multitude of ground submissions and finishes.**

"DOWN AND OUT"
STANDING TO FLOOR JU-JUTSU
TECHNIQUES

Featuring Kevin O'Hagan 6thDan

"50" Throws and takedowns with a multitude of finishing holds and submissions!! Hard to find information and techniques on just one tape (60 mins)

Excellent value at **£14.00**

(Please add £1.00 for postage and packing)

Please make cheques payable to "**Kevin O'Hagan**"
and post to
23 Chester road, St.George, Bristol BS5 7AX

Genuine 60 minutes of action guaranteed

IMPACT JUJUTSU Vol II

The follow on to 'Impact Jujutsu'

This time learn advanced drills, exercises and conditioning routines. Some unique to Kevin O'Hagan and his Ju Jutsu system.

See it all put together in
Freestyle all out sparring too!

IMPACT JUJUTSU Vol II

The new follow up video to the successful
IMPACT JUJUTSU Vol 1

This time **Kevin O'Hagan, 6thDan Jujutsu,** and his senior instructor Paul Flett, take you through a full array of advanced exercises including:

Conditioning, Speed drills, Throws, Padwork, Groundwork drills, Boxing, Vale Tudo (Sparring) and much more…

This tape is a must for anybody serious about training for peak fitness and all round Cross training skills.

Enjoy and learn from this informative and exciting new video available **only** from Kevin O'Hagan.

Excellent value at **£14.00**
(*Please add £1.00 for postage and packing*)
Please make cheques payable to "**Kevin O'Hagan**"
and post to
23 Chester road, St.George, Bristol BS5 7AX

Book review by Geoff Thompson.
Grad. SMA. FSMA

I Thought You'd Be Bigger
A Small person's guide to fighting back.

Kevin O'Hagan is one of the up-and-coming stars of the martial arts in the Nineties. Author of many thought-provoking articles and now his first martial arts book, 'I thought You'd Be Bigger – A Small Person's Guide to Fighting Back' he is one of the highest ranked Ju-Jitsu players in the country today having recently acquired his 6thDan. This book is a result of his life work in Ju-Jitsu and is a very worthy read for anyone, large or small, that is interested in bettering their chances of survival on the pavement arena.

You know, I've worked with violence and violent people all of my adult life and I've learned an awful lot about the human experience and the capacity that our species has to destroy its self over as little as a spilled drink in a bar or eye contact across a busy street: even minor traffic incidents these days seem to be justification enough, to some, to take the life of another human being-it is a hugely violent age that we find seem to find our selves in.

Because our problem on this spinning planet is large, one would automatically presume that it would take a person of equal proportion-i.e. very big- in the physical sense, to deal with or neutralise the problem.
Not so!

At least not from my experience. I have dealt with thousands of violent altercations, I have also had to deal with big men (the odd big woman too!) and faced many life threatening situations, because of this people, when they meet me for the first time, will invariably say in an almost disappointed tone '**Oh! I thought you'd be bigger**.'

What a great title for a book on self defence, if only Kevin O'Hagan hadn't thought of it first and beaten me to the post (Damn!)

Joking aside, it is a brilliant title for a book on self-defence and I can think of no man better qualified to write such a text as my good friend and colleague Kevin O'Hagan.
Not only is it a great title it is also a great book for anyone that thinks size, or lack there off, has any debilitating qualities when it comes to protecting your self and those that you love.

I can tell you categorically that the most ferocious fighters that I have ever worked with have been physically small, like Kevin, but absolute dynamite when the fuse was lit.

I have known Kevin for quite a few years now, not only is he a very personable man he is also a first rate martial artist, one of the few that I really admire and one of even fewer high graded martial artists in Britain that is not afraid to don the white belt and learn off just about anyone that has something of worth to teach.

He is a realist, one of the leaders in the new age of realism, he talks the talk and he walks the walk so I heartily recommend and endorse this text to anyone, of any size or stature, that wants to be better prepared when the metaphoric 'big bad wolf tries to blow your house down.

This is a great book, buy, read it and be bigger for the experience.

Geoff Thompson, Coventry 1998.

A new video from Kevin O'Hagan
"DOWN AND OUT" Vol 2

More dynamic Strikes, throws and submission techniques.

Learn advanced combinations, joint locks, leg locks, chokes, strangles, and much more. This tape is loaded with first class technique.

Modern Combat Jujitsu at it's best

Price £15 inclusive of Post and Packing
Contact Kevin O'Hagan for more details.

"If I wanted to learn something new – this is the video that I would choose. In fact, Kevin O'Hagans videos are the most used tapes in my own personal collection. I have not released any videos of my own because I do not feel I could improve on Kevins instructional tapes!"

Jamie O'Keefe 6th Dan
'Hall of Fame Awardee 1999' , 2001, & 2003
'Founder Fellow of the Society of Martial Arts'.
'Self Protection instructor for Seni 2000, 2001, 2002 Birmingham Expo'

IMPACT JUJUTSU Vol III

PREVENT YOURSELF FROM BECOMING A VICTIM
'Dogs don't know Kung Fu'
A guide to Female Self Protection
By Jamie O'Keefe **£14** including post & packing

Never before has Female Self Protection used this innovative approach to pose questions like. Why do Rapist's Rape? Why are Women abused? Why do Stalkers Stalk? This book takes a look at all Simple, Serious, and Life threatening aspects of Self Protection that concern us daily, along with **PREVENTION** of Child abuse and Child Abduction, Emotional cruelty, Telephone abuse, Road rage, Muggers, Date rape, Weapon attacks, Female abduction, Sexual Assault & Rape, Self defence law, and what it will allow us to do to protect ourselves, plus much more. With over 46,500 words, 77 pictures and 200 printed pages 'Dog's Don't Know Kung fu' is a no nonsense approach to women's self defence. It covers many realistic scenarios involving Children's abduction as well as typical attacks on women. Besides quoting actual events, the book explains how to avoid trouble and how you should react if you get into a situation.

This book is a 'must read' for all women and parents.

It is also important for teenage women, but, due to some of its graphic depiction's of certain incidences, parents should read it first and decide if it's suitable for their child.

Foreword

Dogs don't know kung fu

I'm not usually known for writing forewords to books on self protection, and not because I'm afraid of competition, on the contrary, the more people offering good advice in the fight for better protection be better:- rather its because most of what I read on the subject is crap.

I would never be happy putting my name to something that does not represent my own views, and that's putting it mildly. Not only are the proffered 'self defence' techniques in these manuals unlikely, they are also, very often, dangerous and opinionated.

I have written some 20 books to date on self protection and related subjects so you'd think that there would be very little left for me to learn. I rarely if ever find a manuscript that inspires me or even one that offers something new, a fresh perspective, an innovative approach.

Jamie's book did all the latter. He offered inspiration and sensible (and in retrospect, obvious) solutions to the many enigmatic 'grey areas' that had long perplexed me, a so called expert.

Questions that I have been pondering upon for years were answered at the first reading of this text. So I not only commend Mr O'Keefe on writing probably the best self protection book for women on the market but I also thank him for filling in the gaps in what is, at best, a very intangible subject.

What makes this book even more unique is that Jamie is a veteran instructor with thousands of hours of women's self protection under his belt, he is also an empiricist in that he has put his training to work in real life situations. Now while this may not say a lot to the lay man/woman, to those in the know, it speaks volumes.

Most of the instructors out there teaching self protection have never been in a real situation and so garnish unreal scenarios with un-workable, hypothetical technique.

You will get no such balderdash from this cutting edge instructor. What is offered on the menu in this text will prepare you, of that I have no doubt.

Self protection in the very violent 20th century must now, out of necessity be viewed as an environmental seat belt, it can no longer be down graded as a recreational pastime that comes third down the list of priorities after basket weaving, people are being attacked and killed, every day of the week, in un-provoked, un-solicited and bloody attacks.

My advice to you the reader is to take on board what Jamie has to offer as preventive measures and make them part of your life. Being aware will help you to avoid the majority of attack scenarios, for those that fall outside the periphery of avoidance, the simple, yet effective physical techniques on offer in this book will, if employed with conviction, help to neutralise even the most ardent of attackers.

This is a great book that makes great sense.

The best of its kind.

Geoff Thompson. Coventry 1996

BOUNCERS - SECURITY
DOOR SUPERVISORS
THIS IS THE BOOK THAT TELLS IT ALL

No matter what position you hold in your workplace.
The actions of **Security**
will affect your safety and that of the general public.

Do you really know all you should about
Door Supervisors?

**Find out how much
Door supervisors
should know - but don't know!**
If you want professionalism from your Door Supervisors, you must read this book

If you want to become a Door Supervisor
You should read this book!
If you are a Door Supervisor, Security, or Bouncer,
You must have this book!
No matter how long you have worked the doors – you will learn something from this book

Peter Consterdine said
'This book is a blueprint for the future'

Foreword

Old School – New School

Whether you want to call them Bouncers, Doormen or Door Supervisors, they are still the people with the most thankless job I know.

Constantly under pressure from their own employers, local authorities, the police and especially the general public, it is no wonder that on occasions their self control is taxed to its ultimate. At times, even the best can lose that fine sense of perspective that allows them, night after night to take the constant barrage of banal and often alcohol influenced verbals whilst still keeping the smile in place.

I'd like to think that even going back some 23 years when I first started working on the doors that I subscribed to the "**new school**" approach so creativity described in Jamie's latest book. At that time I weighed eleven and a half stone at six foot one and despite having been on the Gt. Britain and England Karate Teams for some years I knew my traditional marital arts had limited value in the very particular conditions one finds in a night-club.

My weapons were politeness, humour, intellect and large doses of patience and, at times, even larger doses of pre-emptive strikes when occasion demanded. I'm the first to admit, however, that the conditions which applied in the seventies are different to today.

I saw the change begin in the eighties when, as a club owner, it was apparent that the nature of violence, the carrying of weapons, even handguns and the influence of drugs, was going to exact a heavy toll and so it has.

Twenty years ago when someone threatened to come back and shoot me, I slept easy knowing that the next day he wouldn't even remember where he had been the night before - now you'd be reaching for the ballistic vest.

Gang warfare, drugs, control of doors, protection rackets are all now part of the club scene and in the middle is today's doormen. Some are corrupt, some are vicious, some are plain thick, but the majority are honest, well intentioned and keen to do a good job in the face at mounting pressure from many quarters and increased violence and all this with "officialdom" now peering over their shoulder.

Often lied to by the police as to their correct rights of self defence under the law. This book should re-educate people about not only the law, but the many other complex issues.

Expected to be amateur psychologists and perfect man managers versed in a whole range of conflict resolution skills, doormen are still on the 'front line', both male and female.

Door licensing schemes are supposedly the answer to the problems inherent in the profession, but they only go part way to solving many of the issues which still give cause for concern.

Old School, New School clearly defines the gulf between the two approaches as to how the work should be carried out and it should be obligatory reading not only for all door people, but also the police and anyone who has an interest in the leisure industry. By doing so they will get a very clear and honest idea about the difficulties of this work.

Old School, New School isn't just a book about doorwork. It is an effective manual on modern methods of conflict resolution. Over the past few years there has been a substantial rise in the number of companies specialising in delivering courses on conflict resolution in the workplace.

If you read this book you will have all the answers to the management of conflict and aggression.

Doormen have been doing this for years, the only difference being the fact that they have developed their skills from intuition and experience of interpersonal skills in often very violent and aggressive environments.

Now we know that this is a science just as any other form of social interaction and **'Old School, New School'** sets out to educate on the complexities of what is required.

The book recognises, however, that learning these very specialised skills will still not be any guarantee that you can create a person who can be capable of operating in this increasingly dangerous environment. The job is harder now than it ever was and don't let anyone tell you otherwise. Doing this job puts you under a microscope and an official one at that. `Big Brother' most certainly watches over your shoulder and, many would submit, quite rightly so.

I know many doormen who should have no part to play in the industry and many people to whom the recent changes will be hard to adjust to. What I know for a certainty is that the inherent dangers of the work increase every year.

For those doormen and the people who control them to resist the pressure from others to become another drugs distribution outlet takes courage and confidence from everyone in the organisation. Many crumble and give in to the pressure and violence, but equally many don't and I hope that **Old School, New School** will give people not involved in this work, a clear insight for once, the dangers and complexity of the work. For those people who are in the thick of it, I believe that this book is a "blueprint" for the future.

Peter Consterdine

7th Dan Chief Instructor – British Combat Association

Author of :

The Modern Bodyguard

Fit to Fight

Streetwise

What makes tough guys tough?
The Secret Domain

WHAT MAKES

TOUGH GUYS
TOUGH
The Secret Domain
by Jamie O'Keefe

Written by Jamie O'Keefe

Jamie O'Keefe has interviewed key figures from boxing, martial arts, self-protection, bodyguards, doorwork, military, streetfighting and so on. Asking questions that others were too polite to ask but secretly wanted to know the answers.

Interviews include prize-fighter **Roy Shaw**, also **Peter Consterdine, Geoff Thompson,** and **Dave Turton** from the countries leading self-protection organisations 'The British Combat Association' and the 'Self Defence Federation.' Along with Boxing heroes **Dave 'Boy' Green** and East London's former Commonwealth Champion '**Mo Hussein.**' **Plus unsung heroes from the world of Bouncers, Foreign Legion, Streetfighters, and more.**

This book also exposes the Secret Domain, which answers the question 'What makes tough guys tough.'

Find out what some of the toughest guys on the planet have to say about 'What makes tough guys tough' and how they would turn you into a tough guy.

Available from NEW BREED at £14 inc p&p

FOREWORD
DAVID TURTON 7th DAN GOSHINKWAI COMBAT
SENIOR INSTRUCTOR..
BRITISH COMBAT ASSOCIATION

When I was asked by Jamie to write a foreword to this, his latest book, I was both pleased & honoured, and a little intimidated by the prospect.

The first seemingly obvious thing I did, was to read it..

Sounds obvious, but I mean **REALLY** read. On doing so, I found myself being drawn quite deeply into Jamie's thoughts and ideals.

Jamie tends to venture into fields that few, if any, other authors have entered. In doing so, he lays open many often-unanswered questions. He makes those of you-who have asked themselves these soul searching questions, feel that they are not alone.

Having known Jamie for more years than both of us care to remember, I have the advantage of being able to 'hear' his voice, whilst reading his words. I can hear the inflections that show his passion in his beliefs, and the sheer sense of honesty of his words.

Read this book with no other distractions, and give it the respect of doing so with your full attention. Only then the effort will be rewarded with the insight you will get.

I first met Jamie 0'Keefe around twenty years ago. I was a Guest Instructor on an All-Styles self-defence course, and Jamie was a participant on the course, a very noticeable one at that.

I thought here was a talented Karate-Ka, a bit brash, but Oh, so very eager to learn. He was mainly into what we thought of as 'Free-style' Karate back then, but searching for something more. His thirst for learning was nearly insatiable. His Black Belt status was of no real consequence to him. He simply wanted to get stuck in and learn.

He's still doing just that. ... **THE SAME ENTHUSIASM IS PARAMOUNT IN HIS WRITINGS.**

I have looked for a way to go past the usual platitudes, and try to give; what I feel is an honest appraisal of what I feel Jamie is trying to give.... Then it registered ... That's the word ... **HONEST**.. That's the man and his writings.

Jamie always 'tells it like it is'. No holds barred, and no respecter of the many fragile Egos so prevalent in the Martial Arts these days. In this, he ranks along my two other favourite HONEST Combat Authors ... Geoff Thompson and Peter Consterdine.

Don't read this book for 'ways to do it', Don't read this book and be offended by his honesty. Read it, because NOT to read it, will leave a massive hole in your understandings of the World of Man & Violence.

Make it part of your collection, but keep going back to it to read it again and again.

I RECOMMEND THIS BOOK,
I DON'T RECOMMEND MANY... **'READ IT'**

DAVID TURTON 7th DAN GOSHINKWAI COMBAT.

How would you like to be able to
Stop an attack in its tracks?

How would you also like to be able to do it
within a second or two?

How would you like to do it without even
having to draw a breath?

Finally, would you like to know what the
alternative to grappling is?

Then get

'Pre-emptive strikes for winning fights'
'The alternative to grappling'

by
Jamie O'Keefe

Pre-emptive strikes
for winning fights
'The alternative to grappling'

by
Jamie O'Keefe
£14 inc P&P
from
New Breed
Po Box 511
Dagenham, Essex RM9 5DN

Foreword
Pre-Emptive Strikes

On first meeting Jamie O'Keefe, I was struck by his warmth and humour. I was then struck by his fists, head, & knees... Having been on the receiving end (though thankfully only in training) I can attest to the extreme effectiveness of the techniques he teaches. However, as I got to know him better, I was even more impressed by his integrity, honesty and commitment to teaching. Like many of the finest instructors and toughest fighters, Jamie is a gentleman.

These days I consider Jamie a good friend, but that's not why I agreed to write this forward. I believe he writes some of the best material available on modern self-protection, material, which can be, quite literally, life-saving.

I am proud to be able to associate my name with such valuable work

So what is the value in devoting a whole book to the pre-emptive strike?

Be in no doubt that this is one of the most important concepts for personal protection you will ever learn. Over the years I have read about, trained with and worked the door with many individuals who have vast experience of real violence. Every single one of them *without exception* recommends and uses the pre-emptive strike as the prime tactic for self-protection when a physical assault seems inevitable.

This book thoroughly dissects the theory, training and practical application of the pre-emptive strategy. From legal and moral ramifications to pre-attack indicators, from action triggers to Jamie's unique 'Strike Storage & Retrieval System', this book is the most exhaustive, insightful and thought-provoking treatise on the subject I have yet seen.

The lessons contained within these pages were learned the hard way, with spilt, blood & broken bones - this book was written so you don't have to take that route.

Read, absorb, and live by Jamie's advice. You'll be stronger and safer for it.

When talk fails and escape is impossible or impractical, the pre-emptive strike is your best option. I'll let Jamie tell you why.

Simon James
Instructor, Close Quarter Combat Systems

THUGS MUGS AND VIOLENCE

Want to know what its like
when it really kicks off?

Forget the movies - this is the REAL world.

Jamie O'Keefe

www.newbreedbooks.co.uk

Thugs, mugs and violence
The story so far

In this true account of his journey, Jamie O'Keefe unveils the reality of living in the East End of London. From childhood to adult this compelling, harrowing and often highly amusing story tells of his encounters with streetfighting, crime, drugs, violence and the martial arts. It goes through the trials and tribulations of boyhood right through to his days of working on the door in the heart of London's nightlife. Read how each of his confrontations and experiences have played a major part in making him the well respected authority in the fighting arts that he is today.

This book is sure to intrigue and fascinate you so much it will be hard to put it down..

The names and places have been changed in order to protect the guilty

 The late Reg Kray telephoned me from prison, after having just undergone eye surgery to talk through the foreword for the re-print of this book. Due to time restraints and the restrictions that he is bound by, I asked him if he could sum up his thoughts, on this book in a lone paragraph, rather than a lengthy foreword. Although Reg has given me his consent to quote him in length on all the good things that he has said about this book. I have decided to just go with the lone paragraph which was written by Reg himself. *'Thugs mugs and violence'* now has a permanent place within the cell of Reg Kray and is also read by the other inmates.

Thank you Reg for you phone-calls, sometimes three a day, to share your thoughts, ideas, opinions and philosophies with me.

Your friend
Jamie

"Jamie's book 'Thugs, Mugs and Violence' is an insight into the violent times of today and should be read" **Reg Kray – Kray Twins**

Photograph kindly supplied to me for inclusion by Reg Kray

REG KRAY – 32 YEARS SERVED 1968 – 2000 HM Prison.

The latest book by Jamie O'Keefe
NEW BREED PUBLISHING £14 inc P&P
PO BOX 511, DAGENHAM, ESSEX RM9 5DN

NO ONE FEARS WHEN ANGRY!
The Psychology of CONFRONTATION

Roy 'Pretty Boy' Shaw
And
Jamie O'Keefe
(Photo taken from book)

Jamie O'Keefe
Positive Role Model
And Author of
'No One Fears when angry'
An inspirational book on how to
deal with your own Anger and
that of others.

£14 inclusive of P&P
NEW BREED PUBLISHING £14 inc P&P
PO BOX 511, DAGENHAM, ESSEX RM9 5DN

The new book by Alan Charlton

Awareness
Fears
And
Consequences

An insight to understanding what
you
can do to stay safe.
You may have only one chance and
only one choice

By Alan Charlton

NEW BREED PUBLISHING £14 inc P&P
PO BOX 511, DAGENHAM, ESSEX RM9 5DN

Forward
By
Darrin Richardson B.Sc. CMS

I have known Alan Charlton for many years, I have trained with him taught and been taught by him. He is undoubtedly one of the jewels in the art of self-protection in the United Kingdom. In well over 28 years I have seen many instructors, not all can live up to their reputation. Alan however is one. He has trained with some very notable instructors learning his art and developing his own approach to the subject matter. He like many of his kind did not wake up one day an expert instructor, practitioner and author, His skills have developed over many years, and some two years ago he decided to write down many of the lessons he has learnt.

In today's society we live with the fact that we may at anytime be exposed to some sort of violence. This is not just a statement to scare you it is an every day occurrence; all you need to do is open your local paper or watch your local news. It's out there for all to see, just staring you right in the face.

Awareness, fears and Consequences are your Highway Code. We all read the Highway Code before we take our driving tests; we don't remember it all (well I don't) but we do remember the basics. It is those basics that help us drive round in relative safety.

It's the same with Self-protection; Alan Charlton has waded through all the unnecessary ideas and skills that have become the myth of the martial arts and self-defence. We the reader can quickly learn many valuable lessons from this book, without the pain of having first hand experience. This book is crammed full of information and humour and is a must for the library of those who take the subject seriously.

Darrin Richardson 4th Dan

Please feel free to review any of our books on
www.amazon.co.uk
Why not also look at the dedicated websites of the
New Breed Authors

Jamie O'Keefe
www.newbreedbooks.co.uk

Kevin O'Hagan
www.bristolgoshinjutsu.com

Alan Charlton
www.spa.ukf.net

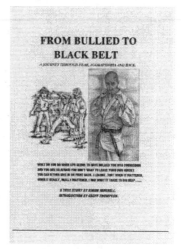

FROM BULLIED TO BLACK BELT
BY SIMON MORRELL
From New Breed, Po box 511
Dagenham, Essex RM9 5DN
£14 inc Post and packing

BAD TO THE BONE
Exploring the many facets of violence
and aggressive behaviour

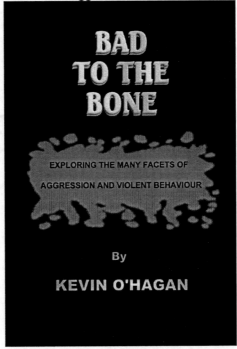

£14 inc Post and packing

IMPACT JUJUTSU Vol III

If you enjoyed this book why not order the other titles currently available from

Jamie O'Keefe
And
Kevin O'Hagan

THEY ARE AN IDEAL PRESENT
IF YOU WANT TO
GIVE SOMETHING DIFFERENT AND SPECIAL

If you borrowed this book and would like your
own copy, write to
Kevin O'Hagan

(Get Kevin to sign and personalise your copy)

Your Advert, Book, Video or Company could be featured here plus in our other books

NEW BREED PUBLISHING

- Do you want to advertise in our books?
- Do you want to become an outlet for our books?
- Do you want to become an agent for us?
- Do you want to join our mailing list?
- Do you want to organise a course or Seminar with one of our Authors?
- Do you want to speak to or meet one of our Authors?

We can work together!

New Breed Publishing

www.newbreedbooks.co.uk

Or in writing to

**New Breed
Po box 511
Dagenham
Essex RM9 5DN
England**

VIDEO MAGAZINE

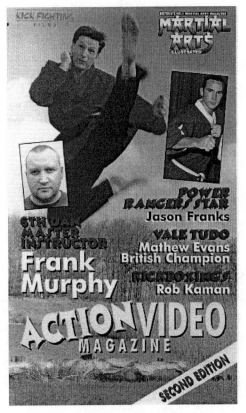

Video No2 features an interview
With Jamie O'Keefe
About his books

Available from
Martial Arts Illustrated
Telephone 01484 435011 for price and ordering details
*Note: This is **not** Jamie's forthcoming
'Pre-emptive strike video'

Combat
Magazine

Available from
Temple Publishing
Tel: 0121 3443737
And all newsagents

A NEW BOOK
AVAILABLE NOW

£14 from
NEW BREED
Or even better
Buy it direct from Kevin O'Hagan
And ask him to autograph it!

Foreword

When I was asked by Kevin to write the foreword to this, Kevin's third book, I was both honoured and surprised. Honoured, because it is a great privilege to write for such an esteemed leader in the field of self-protection. Surprised because, although I have trained and practised various styles for many years, the last four with the Bristol Goshin Jutsu Combat Academy, I am, by no means, an authority on self-protection or the martial arts. I was simply a student of Kevin's who happened also to be criminal defence lawyer. What then could I, a humble lawyer, possibly have to contribute to a book on self-protection by this renowned exponent of the art?

A clue was found in the foreword to Kevin's first book, I Thought you'd be Bigger, which along with his second book, In Your Face, holds pride of place on my bookshelf. In that book, Geoff Thompson, describing Kevin as a 'first rate martial artist' stated that Kevin was one of the few highly graded martial artists who is not afraid to learn from just about anyone that has something of worth to share. This insight into Kevin's personality is precisely what makes him a truly inspirable instructor and self-protection expert. Unlike many mainstream styles whose techniques would be more at home in 17th century Japan, Kevin looks to the streets and people of today's inner cities for inspiration for his own unique and brutally effective style.

Samurai swords do not feature greatly on the streets - bottles, knives and heavy boots do - and Kevin knows it! And unlike many other styles, Kevin doesn't teach techniques as individual acts, but rather he advocates a manner of self-protection that is both fluid and responsive to the environment.

Kevin refers to the techniques of his style as parts of a jigsaw puzzle, each piece (technique) part of a larger whole. If the attacker doesn't respond to one technique, then you move into another.

In this way, each of us was taught to respond to what was physically happening, not to hope that the attacker did this or that and execute the technique regardless. Again, this is the real world - no formal rituals, no time to think. Every technique that Kevin teaches is designed to deal with a real life, in your face, situation.

And with each technique that I learnt and practised, I could see, in my opponent, the faces of the defendants that I saw in court each day (no offence to any of my opponents intended!). And that's how I came to be asked to write this foreword.

You see, as a criminal defence, lawyer, I spent years in police stations, prisons and courts representing the very kind of people that Kevin's style is designed to defend against - real-life murderers, muggers, rapists and robbers. In the evenings, I would attend Kevin's classes and I would delight in telling him, just after he had demonstrated an attack and how to deal with it, 'Yeah, that's the kind of attack that my client used the other night on some poor bastard in the city centre'. I would delight in it because I knew that it meant that what we were doing was real. This wasn't 17th century Japan stuff. This was real-world, real-time self-protection. I'd be thinking that this is what could have happened to me last night if I'd been in the same place, at the same time, as the particular victim that my client had chosen. Kevin was an enthusiastic listener and was always very interested to know the details. Each day that I sat in court, I would hear tales of violence and intimidation perpetrated by thugs and muggers and every time I would hear the details of what they did, I could see in my mind how Kevin's style and training, had it been known to the victim, would have enabled him or her to turn that threat around and put the attacker on the back foot, (or indeed, as with most of Kevin's techniques, on the ground in pain!).

As a lawyer, I had the unique opportunity, unavailable to most students of self-protection, of spending hours talking with my clients, probing them on what they did, and how they chose their victim. And what I learnt from these people is what I can contribute to this book.

I can tell you, without hesitation, that there is not one technique that Kevin teaches that is unrealistic nor one attack that he drills each student, or reader of this book, to protect him or herself against, that has not been used in real life somewhere on the streets of Britain last night or that will not be tried again tomorrow by some thug. What you will read and learn in the following pages, happens. People are knocked to the ground. People are kicked senseless on the streets.

I have seen so many victims in court, who, if only they knew how to effectively protect themselves and to grapple once on the ground, could have saved themselves a beating. If you end up on the ground on the street it is a whole lot different to a competition arena. You will need to know tactics and techniques within this text to save yourself a trip to hospital or worse!

Read this book. What you will learn from it is 'reality' of the streets and how to survive.

Matthew Adkins, Solicitor, 1999

A Foot in the Door
Tony Simpson

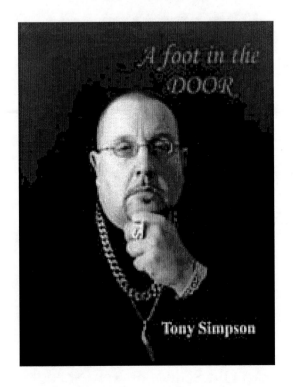

An Old School or New School
Doorman? (you decide)
£14
From
New Breed

Trust me I'm a Doorman
Kev Fisher

An Old School or New School
Doorman? (you decide)
£14
From
New Breed

**Do you have access to the Internet?
If so – why not write a review on this book**

Go to

www.amazon.co.uk

**Under <u>authors</u> search for
Jamie O'Keefe or Kevin O'Hagan**

**Then type in your review or comments
about any of Jamie's or Kevin's books
for the whole world to see!**

**Tip: Write up your review before you go
on line - then cut and paste your review,
which will make a great saving on your
phone bill…**

**To let us know about the review you
submitted so that we can write back and
personally thank you!**

**The new Multimedia CD Rom from
MAD FRANKIE FRASER**
That charts the life of one of Britain's
Most violent men

Telephone: **020 7837 5307**
www.madfrankiefraser.co.uk

Customer Info!

For Credit card orders please buy you books via

www.amazon.co.uk

Amazon will also take international orders.

To order by Cheque or Postal order

Please order direct from the relevant author or from
NEW BREED PUBLISHING
Po box 511
Dagenham
Essex RM9 5DN

If you order direct from author you can also get them to include a personalised message and sign the book!

Peirpaolo Francia

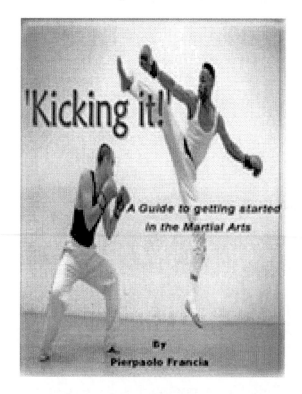

Kicking It!
A Guide to getting started in Martial Arts.
NOW SOLD OUT IN THE UK
But available direct from
pierpaolo2000@yahoo.com

Other books to check out!

Hard Bastards 2
By Kate Kray

Streetfighters
By Julian Davies

Bouncers
By J. Davies & T. Currie

Websites to check out
www.geocities.com/unlicensed2000

www.4-site.co.uk/goshin

www.scoozi.co.uk/sdf

www.spa.ukf.net

www.geocities.com/slthomas316

www.womens-selfdefence.co.uk

www.madfrankiefraser.co.uk

www.thekrays.co.uk

www.royprettyboyshaw.com

www.katekray.com

www.bronsonmania.com

STREETFIGHTERS

JULIAN
DAVIES

REAL FIGHTING MEN TELL THEIR STORIES

New Breed Publishing is becoming a platform for new and upcoming writers who have something to say about the world of violence and how we can deal with it.

We attract readers and writers from:-

Self Defence – Self Protection – Boxing – Street fighting – Combative Fighting Arts – Security – Bouncers – Door Supervisors – and those that have just had a life that's a bit different to the norm!

It is the aim of New Breed publishing to give you, the reader, an insight into a world that lies hidden beneath the glossy world of safety that we know as our comfort zone.

Although you will not find any 'Authors' within New Breed. You will find real people that can write about reality and hopefully advise you on how to lead a better violent free life.

Thank you for reading this book and I hope you with go on to check out the other books available from New Breed Publishing.

Regards and respect
Stay Safe

Jamie O'Keefe

Books related to
Positive Outcomes and good Role Models

Our Website www.newbreedbooks.co.uk is dedicated to publications from unusual authors writing about areas of their life that aim to inspire into taking a positive path in life.

They are people who have not come from privileged backgrounds. People who have had to face fear, hardship and make life choices that are hard to imagine possible.

At New Breed we do not involve ourselves with Sport, Politics or Religion and will not attempt to make choices for you or judge you on your personal preferences or life's choices..

Our aim is to provide you with hard to find information via our books, in the hope that it will enable you to make a better informed choice on life saving decisions, rather than as you may do now through reactional habit.

Our aim is also to help you understand the full consequences, risk and dangers that are associated with challenging behavior which surrounds us all in our everyday lives.

Our site contains advice from men and women who have had to deal with threat and violence and have come out the other end to tell their tale.

Although some have suffered great pain and loss throughout their life experiences, they have picked themselves back up, dusted themselves down, and have become stronger individuals who are self enabled to get on with their lives.

We hope that our books will expose the seedier and nasty world of physical, mental and verbal attacks, in order for you to avoid the same experiences that some of our authors have. We enable you to put your toes in the water without you having to get wet or drowned.

Although these books are written mainly by people experienced in Door work, security, and fighting related arts. They are 'people' who have chosen to share the reasons that they have chosen the good path in life.

New Breed Publishing operates as a platform for positive people promoting positive outcomes, who refuse to accept the hand they were dealt in life.

If you want to join us and take steps towards making your environment a safer and better place to be. Come on in and see what's on offer..

Welcome to our world.

Jamie

EXTREME DEFENCE
Tough measures for dangerous situations

Welcome to the reality of street self defence with "Extreme Defence" This video tape gives you no-nonsense, no-holds barred responses against a multitude of dangerous and potentially life threatening situations. Witness fast, hard and rapid fire techniques as tough and uncompromising as the Pavement Arena itself. Learn revolutionary scenario based drills and training methods to improve and enhance your fighting skills for survival. Become your own Bodyguard!

This is the final word on effective and practical techniques in the ever increasing "Reality Revolution". If you are interested and serious about Street Self Defense and Close Quarter Combat that really works under extreme conditions, this tape is an absolute must!

Brought to you by Renowned Self Protection Instructor, Author and Submission Fighting competitor – Sensei Kevin O Hagan of The Bristol Goshin Jutsu Combat Academy

Warning
Due to the nature of some of this tape's content, it cannot be sold to persons under 18 years old.
For Details Phone : 0117 952 5711
Or E-mail : cannon@bristolcity24.freeserve.co.uk

198

SUDDEN IMPACT

No Holds Barred Fighting and Mixed Martial Arts Training

Brought to you by renowned Trainer, Fighter and Author
Kevin O Hagan

Following in the footsteps of his successful Impact Ju Jutsu tapes, comes his latest video "Sudden Impact" which puts together all of the ideas, drills and training methods from his previous "Impact Series" into a complete picture.
Watch Kevin and his guys working out at his famed "Impact Gym" in his NHB Classes. Witness hard conditioning, Vale Tudo focus mitt drills, stand up sparring, ground sparring and "All In" No Holds Barred sparring.
This video covers special drills for fight preparation and conditioning! Full clips of Live fights, tactics, tips and interviews are all included.

This tape is packed with proven and workable, reality based training for the Mixed Martial Arts Fighter, trainer or enthusiast. Every thing you see is real, live and spontaneous!

Price £15.00 inc P and P (UK)
    £18.00 inc P and P (Overseas)

Send a cheque or Postal Order made Payable to Kevin O Hagan to:

23, Chester Road
St George
Bristol
BS5 7AX   For more details phone 0117 952 5711 or E-mail cannon@bristolcity24.freeserve.co.uk